Origins of Chinese Art and Craft

Compiled by **Li Xiaoxiang**
Illustrated by **Fu Chunjiang**

⚓ **ASIAPAC** • **SINGAPORE**

Publisher
ASIAPAC BOOKS PTE LTD
996 Bendemeer Road #06-09
Singapore 339944
Tel: (65) 6392 8455
Fax: (65) 6392 6455
Email: asiapacbooks@pacific.net.sg

Come visit us at our Internet home page
www.asiapacbooks.com

First published April 2002 as *Origins of Chinese Folk Arts*
(ISBN 981-229-264-0)

This revised edition
First published January 2006

© 2006 ASIAPAC BOOKS, SINGAPORE
ISBN 981-229-441-4

Cover illustrations by Fu Chunjiang
Cover design by Wong Seow Wee
Page layout by Wong Seow Wee
Body text in 11pt Times New Roman
Printed in Singapore by FuIsland Offset Printing (S) Pte Ltd

Publisher's Note

"Chinese arts and handicrafts have exerted a considerable impact on our imagination with their extraordinary styles. They are artworks that combine the boldest innovation and the most refined aesthetic tastes. We are moved and shocked by, and cannot help admiring, the mysterious ambience surrounding this long isolated realm of art. They exhibit the outstanding talent of a nation and have left an indelible mark on human history."

This is the comment made by French President Jacques Chirac on Chinese arts and handicrafts in a lecture given at Shanghai Tongji University in December 2004.

In fact, of all human professions and vocations, manual labour is the one that can enable us to embrace nature to the full. Chinese handicrafts, which have evolved their own unique attractions over the past thousands of years, have become a splendid treasure of Chinese culture.

The first edition of this book has been well received by our readers. We have made partial revisions for this new edition in order to enhance their reading pleasure.

Firstly, we retain the popular comic style that combines information and entertainment, and add some new stories and illustrations. Secondly, two entirely new sections are added that focus on Chinese bronzes and jades. Thirdly, the section on recreation in the first edition is removed. We are going to expand that subject into a separate book.

We would like to take this occasion to thank Ms Li Xiaoxiang and Asiapac editors for their joint editorial work. Thanks also go to Mr Yang Liping for his translation of the newly added parts, and Mr Fu Chunjiang for his vivid comics and illustrations. We would also like to thank the production team for their contribution.

About the Compiler

Li Xiaoxiang 李小香 was born in 1946. After graduating from Hunan Normal University in 1969, she taught Chinese language and literature in a high school. Later, she worked in Zhejiang University as a staff member of the Higher Education Research Department, an Office Administrator in the Economics Department, and as editor of an academic journal.

Besides having a firm foundation in Chinese language and literature, Li is also skilled in editorial work. She has a deep understanding of traditional Chinese culture, especially Buddhism, and has penned several discourses on this subject.

With her penchant for writing, she has produced 20-odd literary pieces and works on various topics. Her published works for the children's market include *The Story of Xinqiji*, *The Story of a Junior Barber*, *The Story of a Fisherman and a Goldfish*, and *Wisdom in Chinese Proverbs*.

She is presently a Senior Editor with Wuhan University Press.

About the Illustrator

Fu Chunjiang 傅春江 born in 1974, is a native of Chongqing municipality in Southeastern China's Sichuan province. He has been fond of drawing ever since childhood and graduated in Chinese language studies. Fu loves traditional Chinese culture and has tried his hand at drawing comics.

Since 1994 he has been drawing comics and his works include *The Story of Kites* and *The Faint-hearted Hero*. He has also participated in the production of *One Riddle for One Story*.

His works like *Golden Rules for Business Success, Origins of Chinese Festivals* and *The Chinese Code of Success: Maxims by Zhu Zi* published by Asiapac Books are widely acclaimed.

Foreword

Tens of thousands of years ago, the eastern part of the northern hemisphere was a wide expanse of land which was populated by a group of people. They learnt to gather wood and make fires. They started to hunt, fish and farm. They invented written text. They created culture. They established a nation.

They were the earliest Huaxia people who prospered and multiplied to become the largest ethnic group on Earth. They developed by leaps and bounds to forge a dazzling culture. Many a brilliant ancient civilisation has been swallowed up by the currents of time, but the Huaxia culture has managed to survive. In fact, it continues to exert its influence today, not only within China, but also beyond, via the Silk Road, migration, etc.

The flames of wars erupted. Dynasties rose and fell. Despite the changing faces of political power, the essence of the Chinese people has remained unchanged.

Today, the Chinese people are not merely an ethnic group, but a larger cultural entity spread all over the world.

The most distinguishing aspect of Chinese culture is its all-encompassing nature. It emphasises justice and moral integrity, human relations, the power of music and rituals to cultivate the hearts of men, and the oneness of Man and Heaven... all at the same time. Next is its wisdom — it engineers invention and change, and is prolific and dynamic. Last but not least is its ingenuity — it is ever progressive and enlightening.

Taking a flying leap into the global lake of the world,
The ancient Chinese culture exudes the vitality of youth!

Li Xiaoxiang
Wuhan University Press

Contents

INTRODUCTION

In this book you will see potteryware that are antique, elegant, functional and aesthetic; ancient jades that are crystal-clear and translucent; bronzes that have fascinated the world with their mystical styles; Chinese silk and embroideries that are made with brilliant techniques; and wax-dyed clothes with facial masks depicting characters in Chinese operas; tiger-head shoes, old-style rattan products, lacquer, cloisonné, etc.

These works of distinct characteristics have won global interest and attraction to their places of origin.

Chinese art and craft originated thousands of years ago. Yet these works of art still benefit our lives considerably. History has shown that Chinese art and craft have played a significant role in promoting the progress of human culture across the world.

Increasingly, China's artistic industries will contribute towards the growth of the global economy and culture. China has developed from being a large producer of silk products to an industry leader in silk-making technologies. She is also the biggest producer and exporter of pottery, with porcelain products exported to over 150 countries, and has carved a name for making one of the finest porcelain in the world.

Combining concise information, appealing illustrations and vivid comics, this book will transport you to the world of these alluring Chinese works of art that have endured the test of time.

POTTERY

China is the native home of pottery and porcelain. Pottery began about 8,000 years ago during the New Stone Age. Many terracotta (红陶) wares were made during the Neolithic Period about 6,000 years ago. Patterns and diagrams in black, white and red were painted on the porcelain. This type of ceramics became known as the Ancient Painted Pottery (彩陶).

The earliest pottery were daily items used to hold food and store rations.

As China is well known throughout the world for its porcelain, which is also known as china, Westerners first got to know about the country because of its porcelain. Eventually, they decided to call the country which produced china China.

A vase with a narrow neck makes a good container for drawing water.

The ceramic tripod where food is cooked in a ceramic bowl.

Pottery

Painted Pottery

Pottery at that time served a functional purpose, but colourful pictures and patterns were also added to them. The artistic standards at that time were pretty high.

Ceramic vases, containers, bowls and plates.

Black Pottery

Other than painted pottery, there was also black pottery. Its walls were very thin and its frame, beautiful. There is another kind of black pottery called the egg-shell pottery where the walls are as thin as an egg shell. The skills and artistic flair involved are simply astounding.

The Legend of God of Pottery

In the beginning, the Earth was flooded and the people had to live in mountain caves. They went down the mountain every day to fetch water. To store the water, they used moistened soil to make water containers.

Crash!

Not again! Be gentle when you put it.

This ware isn't hardy enough.

How come the earth at the bottom of the pit is so firm?

A man called Ning Feng was burning a wild beast in the cave one day.

I see! Earth that has been burnt becomes hardier. I can use it to make containers that aren't so fragile.

Tri-coloured Glazed Pottery

Tri-coloured Glazed Pottery made its appearance during the Tang Dynasty. Tri-coloured Glazed Pottery is a kind of brightly-coloured pottery that uses mainly yellow, green and white colours. Images of people, animals and daily items were commonly seen on Tri-coloured Glazed Pottery. Those with images of horses were the most common and most beautiful. Hence, they were very popular too. Tri-coloured Glazed Pottery was mostly used as burial items. The emperors, royalty and nobles of the Tang Dynasty were buried with Tri-coloured Glazed Pottery.

The ancient art of Tri-coloured Glazed Pottery is still alive in present-day Luoyang and Xi'an. Images of horses, camels and terracotta warriors are very lifelike and popular.

Horses in Tri-coloured Glazed Pottery

Horses were not just a means of transport during the Tang Dynasty. They were also indispensable in the army. Horses were also highly-esteemed animals. The emperors and nobles of the Tang Dynasty loved to keep horses.

Women in Tri-coloured Glazed Pottery
Women were portrayed with bright colours, beautiful forms and expressive faces.

Camels in Tri-coloured Glazed Pottery
The Tang Dynasty enjoyed great diplomatic and trading ties with external parties.
The enduring camels were an important means of transport on the Silk Road.

The Story of Tri-coloured Glazed Pottery

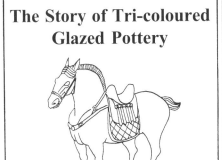

Long ago in Henan, there was a Green Dragon Mountain. At its foot is the Huangye River. The people living by the river made pottery for a living.

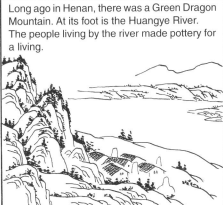

During the Tang Dynasty, a young man called Tao Ge'er saved an old herbalist.

The old man married his daughter, Sancai, to Tao Ge'er.

You'll need this medicine in future. Let this be my daughter's trousseau.

Tao Ge'er and Sancai were a loving couple.

Look at the lovely rainbow. If only I could burn these colours onto the earthenware.

But where could I find the dyes for them?

I know. Give me the medicine my father gave you.

Will applying the medicine on it produce colours on the earthenware?

Just place it in the kiln first.

When it was time to remove them from the kiln...

Ah! They are walking out on their own!

The colours are gorgeous and dazzling. I've never seen such earthenware before.

When Empress Wu Zetian learnt about it, she summoned Tao Ge'er and Sancai into the palace with their painted pottery.

The people and animals on the earthenware started dancing before her.

Only the palace is fit to keep such earthernware.

You'll stay in the palace and make earthenware.

We only hope to work for the commoners.

No way!

Tao Ge'er, let's leave.

With a wave of her hand, the two horses grew in size.

The couple mounted and rode up into the sky with their painted pottery.

Come back here!

What atrocity! I want all pottery workers by the Huangye River to present me with painted pottery!

Your Majesty, this is the painted pottery.

There are only three colours and they can't even move.

It wasn't easy for them to come up with it. I hereby order that such painted pottery is to be exclusive to the palace!

And so this painted pottery became known as Tri-coloured Glazed Pottery.

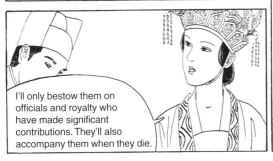

I'll only bestow them on officials and royalty who have made significant contributions. They'll also accompany them when they die.

Porcelain

The making of pottery paved the way for the discovery of porcelain by the Chinese. During the Shang-Zhou period, a green porcelain and a greenish-yellow porcelain made their appearance. After more than 1,500 years of development, the first green porcelain in China was seen in the late Eastern Han Period. Later, people began to produce white and painted porcelain.

Green Porcelain

It is lightly coloured on its surface. The colour could be green or greenish-yellow. It resembles green jade.

White Porcelain

The base and glaze used are both white. Its preparation is more demanding. With white porcelain, the people could add patterns and pictures to it.

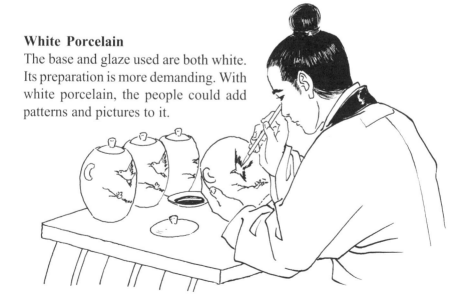

Coloured Porcelain

The white-based porcelain with blue painting on it is the quintessential coloured porcelain. The colour is similar to the paint used in traditional Chinese paintings.

Jingdezhen — the Porcelain Capital of the World

Located in northern Jiangxi Province, Jingdezhen has been known as the "Porcelain Capital of the World" for a long time. During the Eastern Jin Period, its name was Xinpingzhen. During the reign of Emperor Zhenzong (1004-1007) in the Southern Song period, official kilns were set up here and it was decreed that all the porcelain pieces made for the imperial court should be marked "Made in the Jingde Period" because "Jingde" was Emperor Zhenzong's reign title. Thus the town acquired a new name, "Jingdezhen," which has been in use until today. Elegant in shape and unique in style, porcelain products made in Jingdezhen have won the following reputation: "[being] white as jade, clear as a mirror, thin as paper, and sounding as a chime bell." Famille-rose Porcelain, Linglong Porcelain, Blue-White Porcelain, and Colour-Glazed Porcelain constitute its four famous traditional styles. Other well-known styles include Wucai porcelain, Porcelain Sculpture and Botai (thin as egg-shell) Porcelain. Chinese emperors from the Yuan Dynasty through the Qing Dynasty all dispatched special officials to Jingdezhen to supervise the manufacture of royal porcelain products.

The Spread of Porcelain-Making Technologies

Along with its porcelain products sold abroad, Jingdezhen also found its porcelain-making techniques spread to other parts of the world. First, these techniques were introduced to Korea, Japan, Vietnam, Thailand and some Middle Eastern countries, and then made their way to Europe via the Arabs. In addition, many foreigners also paid special visits to Jingdezhen to study its unique techniques.

Thailand: As early as 1299 during the Yuan Dynasty, the Thai emperor sent one of his princes to the capital of the Yuan Dynasty, requesting China to help it make porcelain. Upon the imperial decree, local authorities in Jingdezhen selected a group of senior craftsmen and dispatched them to Thailand where, they came up with the noted Sukhothai Porcelain in cooperation with the local Thai potters.

Vietnam: Vinh Long flourished in the early part of the 16th century because of its adoption of the Jingdezhen porcelain-making techniques, and has since won the epithet of "Jingdezhen of Vietnam."

France: French missionary Pere Francois Xavier D'Entrecolles (1664-1741), with the Chinese name of Yin Hongxu, lived in Jingdezhen for seven years. While spreading Christian doctrines, he also spent time collecting the local porcelain-making techniques, which he introduced to Europe.

Pottery and Porcelain Route

Everyone knows about the Silk Road but did you know that there is also a Pottery and Porcelain Route on the seas of China? From the late Tang Dynasty onwards, a large volume of pottery and porcelain were exported. And that continued for more than 1,000 years. The sea route that transported pottery and porcelain from China to Asia, Africa, Europe and the United States became known as the Pottery and Porcelain Route.

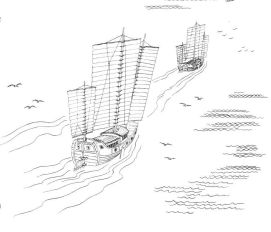

In the beginning, the Europeans regarded chinaware as highly precious. Only the royalty and aristocrats could own them. The value of chinaware was equivalent to gold at that time. Europe even sent artisans to learn the craft from the Chinese.

Yixing, the "Capital of Pottery" — Purple-Clay Pottery

One of the scenic spots in the Tai Lake area, Yixing is known as the Capital of Pottery the world over, boasting a pottery-making history of over 7,000 years. Dating back to the hard pottery with geometrical patterns and primitive celadon, Yixing has kept on improving its pottery-making art. A legend goes that Fan Li and Xi Shi were there to make pottery objects during the Spring and Autumn Period. By the Ming and Qing dynasties, Yingxing pottery reached its peak of reputation both inside China and overseas. Yixing produces mainly daily pottery articles, such as purple-clay pots, plates, cups, bottles, flowerpots and carvings. Sophisticated in texture and plain in decoration, they exhibit distinct national characteristics. It is said that Yixing pottery containers can prevent tea from spoiling in hot summer and protect potted plants from contracting root diseases.

The Story of *Geyao*

Geyao is one of the Five Famous Kilns during the Song Dynasty. It is famous for the crack lines it produces in porcelain.

It is said that there were two brothers who produced porcelain in Longquan, Zhejiang. The people called the elder brother's kiln *geyao* 哥窑 and the younger brother's, *diyao* 弟窑.

Elder Brother has taken away all my business. But my porcelain isn't as good as his. I have to do something.

It's done!

I'll remove them when the temperature has gone down.

Let me get some rest first.

Splash!

If cold water is splashed into the kiln, it'll probably destroy all the porcelain.

It's almost time. Let's open the kiln.

What happened?

None of the porcelain pieces is broken.

Only the outer layer shows some cracks. On second look, the crack lines are pretty nice.

When he sold them, they were very popular with the people.

So beautiful! What porcelain do you call it?

The elder brother learnt something new from this incident. He came up with a way to let the base of the porcelain expand more than the top layer. That created the crack lines without breaking the porcelain. This became the famous cracked porcelain.

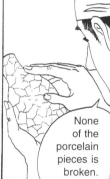
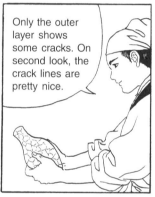

The Making of Pottery and Porcelain

This is a potter's wheel.

You place your foot on the pedal to spin it.

Place some earth in the centre. As you spin the wheel, you add pressure to the centre of the earth.

You gradually pull the sides of the earth upwards.

Add some water at the same time to keep it moist.

This method looks tougher than the coiling method.

This vessel with a small opening is even more difficult to shape.

We often talk about pottery and porcelain. What's the difference between them? Porcelain is made with china and painted over before baking it in high heat. Porcelain is more hardy than earthernware. Though it's not as fine, it looks shiny and doesn't absorb water. It gives a lovely tinkle when you hit it.

SILK

China was the first country in the world to discover silk cocoons. For more than 6,000 years, the Chinese have been breeding silk cocoons. Ancient Greeks knew China as Seres, which meant the Silk Country. When silk was introduced into the Western world, the Westerners fell in love with the beauty of silk. They described it as being as beautiful as a fairy maiden and as mysterious as a dream.

Breeding Silkworms

Cocoon is a type of greyish white fluid which is secreted by the silkworm. It is made up of silk protein and silk glue which hardens upon contact with air. Silk is malleable and elastic. A silkworm can secrete about 1,000 metres of silk thread.

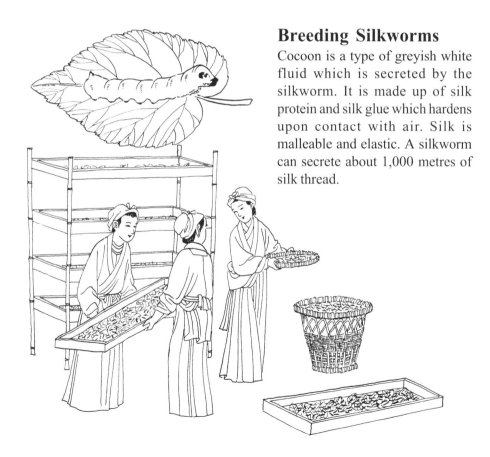

Picking Mulberry Leaves

In one of China's earliest compilations of poems, *Shijing* 《诗经》, picking mulberry leaves was often mentioned. Below is one of the poems:

Planting Mulberry
How beautiful are the mulberry trees
The leaves are full and luscious
Upon seeing my beloved
My heart leaps with joy

As silkworms feed on mulberry leaves, mulberry trees were grown in abundance. The job of picking mulberry leaves was usually left to the womenfolk.

   Characters like *sang* 桑 (mulberry), *can* 蚕 (cocoon) and *si* 丝 (silk) were already found in the earliest Chinese writing — the shell-and-bone writing.

Founder of Silk Weaving

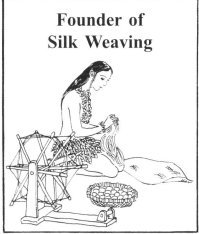

In ancient times, people had no clothes. They used leaves and animal skin to cover their bodies.

There was an elderly man by the surname of Lei. He had a bright and beautiful daughter called Lei Feng. Every day without fail, Lei Feng would pick wild fruit to feed her parents.

But the red mulberry fruit is sour.

Hmm, tastes pretty good! It's fragrant and sweet. Let me pick some home for Father and Mother.

From then on, Lei Feng would pick mulberry fruit every day. One day, she discovered silkworms feeding on mulberry leaves.

After some time…

The other fruit get redder as they ripen. But why does mulberry fruit just get darker?

The silkworms grew day by day. Finally, they began to spit out silk that eventually formed a silk pouch.

Lei Feng took the worms home. They later turned into pupae and then moths.

She bred them and many eggs were laid. These eggs later produced many silkwoms.

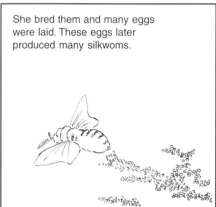

I will use the grown ones to make a silk net.

Lei Feng fed the silkworms with mulberry leaves.

There is so much silk thread! If only I could weave them.

Let's unravel the silk first.

Then weave it into little square pieces.

Now, let's join the square pieces together to form a coat.

Mother, how do you find it?

This was the very first silk clothing ever produced.

It's so nice and warm.

I hear Lei Feng uses the silk from worms to make comfortable clothing.

Really? Let's go and learn from her.

Lei Feng, this is my latest creation.

From then on, everyone started breeding silkworms to make clothing.

When the Yellow Emperor learnt about it, he made Lei Feng his empress. Together, they ruled the country. That paved the way for men to till the lands and for women to weave silk. People then honoured Lei Feng by calling her Mother Lei.

Horse-head Goddess of Silkworm

Besides Mother Lei, the people also worshipped the Horse-head Goddess of Silkworm. The bizarre story goes like this:

There was a father who had to go away, leaving his daughter and his horse alone at home.

If you can bring Father home, I'll marry you.

Not long after, the horse returned with the girl's father on its back.

Did you promise to marry the horse if it brings me home?

Yes.

A few days later, the father saw his daughter wrapped in the horse skin on a big tree. She had already turned into a silkworm with a horse head. She was spitting out white and shiny thread to form a cocoon around her.

The cocoon and silk were larger and better than the usual ones. The quantity was greater too. People then called the tree *sang* (mulberry) and the girl, Horse-head Goddess of Silkworm.

Since ancient times, worshipping the Goddess of Silkworm has been a very important ritual. Even the emperor would personally lead in the ceremony. In some parts of the country, the people would worship the Goddess of Silkworm with pork and porridge on the 15th day of the first lunar month 正月. Why pork and porridge? As rats were said to destroy silk and cocoons, the pork porridge was meant as food for the rats so that they would leave the silkworms and cocoons alone.

Types of Weaving Looms

Weaving looms transform silk cocoons into beautiful silk.

They can be classified into two categories. The first type weaves plain silk fabrics while the other type creates silk cloth with patterns on it.

Yaoji 腰机 *is* the simplest and most primitive type of loom. It weaves simple patterns on the cloth.

Some looms which are as tall as 21 m have to be manned by two people.

This area is the hualou 花楼*. The threads have to be pulled according to the preset pattern.*

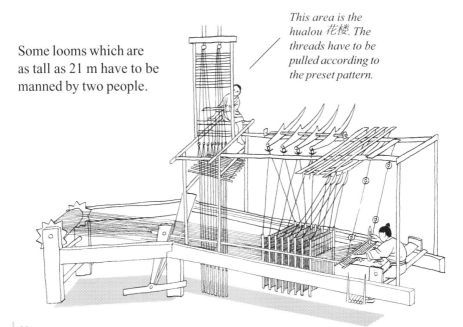

Various Kinds of Silk

Silk is a generic term for silk products. There are many kinds of silk. Below are some examples.

Jin 锦

Its texture is the heaviest and the richest. It is the representative of traditional Chinese silk. This type of silk gives the wearer a sense of pride.

Luo 罗

Its texture is light, making it an ideal choice of fabric for summer.

Ling 绫 (damask silk)

This is a type of ultra-thin silk with patterns. Besides being used in clothing, it is also used in the mounting of calligraphy.

Juan 绢 (tough, thin silk)

This refers to silk products made from unprocessed silk. The fabric is thin yet tough. It is mainly used in the mounting of calligraphy.

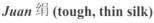

Sha 纱 (gauze)

The grains are criss-crossed. The fabric is light, soft and transparent. The costumes of officials were mostly made with this fabric. The headdress of the officials was known as the black gauze cap, which later came to mean an official post.

The Silk Road

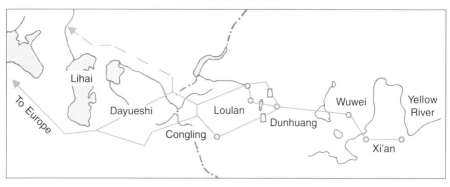

The ancient Silk Road began at Chang'an (known as Xi'an today) and continued through Hexi, Xinjiang, Congling (known as Bomier Highlands today), West Asia and finally Europe, covering a total distance of more than 7,000 km.

Camels, dubbed the sails of the desert, was an important mode of transport along the Silk Road.

From 2 BC to AD 13, the Silk Road remained ancient China's longest international trade route. The name came about because silk enjoyed the highest trade volume and the greatest popularity along this route. The Silk Road was a meeting point for Eastern and Western cultures and served as an important economic bridge.

Other than silk, the goods transported included metalware and lacquerware. Skills were also transmitted via the Silk Road.

Zhang Qian Founded the Silk Road

During the Western Han Period, in a bid to remove the threat of the invading Huns, Emperor Hanwu entrusted Zhang Qian with an important task.

I want you to head for the Western Region and build diplomatic ties with this country called Dayueshi and combine forces with them to attack the Huns.

I will do my utmost.

Zhang Qian and his 100-strong entourage left Xi'an and headed for the Western Region. But the Huns caught them and help them captive for 10 years.

One night, Zhang Qian made his escape.

Though I didn't accomplish the mission I've set out to do, I got to understand the geography, products and the lifestyles of the people in the Western Region.

I believe this will prove useful for Your Majesty.

In AD 119, Zhang Qian made his second envoy trip to the Western Region. This time, he took more than 300 men with him and visited many places in the Western Region.

I've brought silk, satin, metalware and lacquerware from the Central Plains. I've also brought with me various skills and techniques.

Your Excellency, will these seedlings for grapes, pomegranates, walnuts and carrots from the Western Region be of any use to us?

Of course.

Following Zhang Qian's journeys to the Western Region, the Silk Road was used by merchants, peasants, monks and travellers moving between the Central Plains and the Western Region.

The Present-day Silk Road

The Silk Road actually had such an important role in history. I thought it was merely a tourist attraction.

Though the Silk Road is no longer an important trade route, the ancient relics and natural scenery that can be seen along the way still draw large groups of local and overseas visitors.

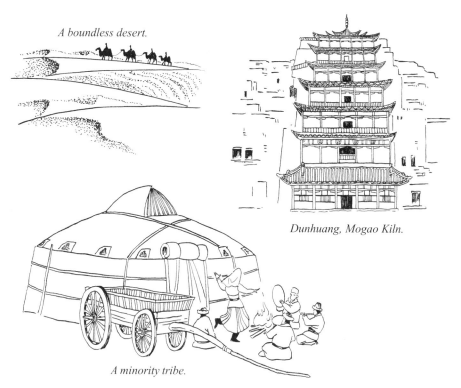

A boundless desert.

Dunhuang, Mogao Kiln.

A minority tribe.

Snow-capped mountains all-year round.

The lush green grasslands.

Terracotta warriors found in
Emperor Qin's Mausoleum.

The ancient
city of Xi'an.

EMBROIDERY

Chinese embroidery is more than just a folk art. It has also been recognised as a world-class form of art. Embroidery has its origins in basic sewing. More than 18,000 years ago, the Upper Cavemen of the Old Stone Age in ancient China had already started using animal bones as needles to sew pieces of animal skin together.

Four Types of Chinese Embroidery

The blueprint for embroidery mainly comes from the works of famous painters. Some are also drafts provided by artists. Embroidery has enjoyed such a great development that every region has its own unique style. Let us look at the four main types.

Suzhou Embroidery

The picture is simple and the embroidery intricate. Its famous works include cats, goldfish and white peacocks.

Hunan Embroidery

The style is simple and the picture true-to-life. Lions and tigers are its traditional subjects.

Su embroidery: pine tree and cranes symbolise longevity.

Xiang embroidery: tiger.

Guangdong Embroidery

It is colourful and boasts many kinds of stitchwork. Traditional subjects are the phoenix heading towards the sun and two dragons playing with a pearl.

Sichuan Embroidery

Pretty and vivid, its traditional subjects are the hibiscus, carp, rooster and cockscomb flower.

Yue embroidery: Flowers and feathers in harmony.

Shu embroidery: Zhuo Wenjun listening to the ancient zither.

Shu embroidery: pandas rollicking on the ground.

The Story of Hunan Embroidery

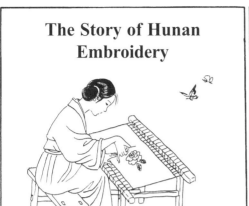

Legend has it that a man called Yuan Qi who lived by the eastern shore of Xiangjiang River had excellent cloth-weaving skills.

He had a daughter called Yuan Mingzhu who had learnt from him since she was young.

Ha, ha! My daughter's skills have surpassed mine.

When Mingzhu turned 13, her mother passed away. Yuan Qi then married a widow by the surname of Li.

Child, call Mother.

Mother.

Argh!

Shortly after Madam Li married Yuan Qi, the latter was bitten by a venomous snake.

Wretched girl! Where did you get the medicine from?

You must have stolen my money. See if I don't beat you to death!

I didn't steal your money! A fairy taught me how to stitch embroidery.

Since embroidery makes such good money, you'll weave cloth in the day and stitch in the night. You're not to leave the room!

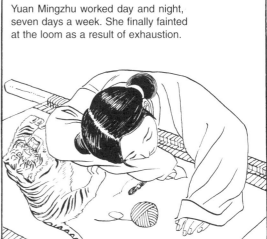

Yuan Mingzhu worked day and night, seven days a week. She finally fainted at the loom as a result of exhaustion.

Madam Li died of shock on the spot.

After Yuan Qi recovered, father and daughter wove cloth and stitched embroidery to make a living. Other girls also started to learn stitching from Mingzhu. And so the skill passed down the generations. To this day, people still talk about how the early embroidery in Hunan was taught by a fairy maiden.

The Story of Xiuniang

Long ago, there was a girl called Xiuniang who was excellent at needlework. Everything she stitched was lifelike. Even the flowers she stitched attracted butterflies. It was amazing!

Hey! Stitch a picture for me.

There was a tyrannical landlord. One day…

The poor have stiff fingers. I'm afraid the images will not turn out well.

Humph! I don't care. I want a portrait of myself ready by tomorrow.

Otherwise, you can forget about making a living in this town!

The next day…

What?!

How come it has neither hair nor beard?

 Good heavens!

 So much gold, silver and jewellery. Not bad!

 It's my love indeed. Ha! Ha!

 Go on in!

 Xiuniang pushed the landlord into the stitched treasure house and shut the door after him.

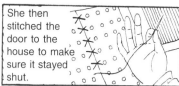 She then stitched the door to the house to make sure it stayed shut.

 You won't be able to harm others anymore.

 From then on, the tyrannical landlord disappeared from the face of the Earth. The young girls in the village all wanted to master Xiuniang's consummate needlework craft.

Embroidery in Daily Life

Embroidery still plays an important role in our everyday life. Many daily necessities such as tapestries, blankets, pillow cases, shoes, hats, pouches, quilt covers, curtains, signages, tablecloths and handkerchiefs have embroidery on them.

China used to be an agricultural country. The men would till the land while the women would weave cloth. From a very young age, women were taught to weave cloth and sew. Embroidery was a must for them. It was a symbol of their chastity. A girl had to sew embroidery on her undergarments, shoes and quilt covers before she got married. They were meant to be proof of her artistic skills. Girls who could not embroider were despised and deemed to be lacking in the virtues of a woman.

Various Kinds of Embroidered Stitchwork

Rong Embroidery 绒绣

Pictures and scenery are stitched on a piece of special mesh cloth using high-quality coloured threads. The colour is rich. Paintings, sofa covers and cushions are items which use this embroidery.

Zhu Embroidery 珠绣

Coloured beads are used. Embroidered shoes with beads are very famous. Handbags, skirts and evening wear with *zhu* embroidery are also very popular.

Tiao Embroidery 挑花

It is also known as "cross stitch". Various crosses are stitched to form a picture.

Appliqué Embroidery

Cloth of different colours and shapes are joined together to form a picture. They are then pasted on a piece of cloth and stitched.

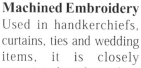

Machined Embroidery

Used in handkerchiefs, curtains, ties and wedding items, it is closely associated with modern living and is very popular.

There is also another kind of amazing embroidery which uses human hair. In ancient days, as an expression of their devoutness, Buddhists would use their hair to sew images of Buddha and Goddess of Mercy.

JADE

Jades are an important part of traditional Chinese culture. They have enchanted, with their entrancing beauty and overflowing warmth, the hearts of emperors, ministers as well as ordinary people over the past 5,000 years.

Jade perfume bag (Qing Dynasty)

Opinions have been divided as to the purposes and functions of jade objects. Some say they were used in religious and ritual ceremonies; others consider them ornaments for wearing and appreciating, which indicated the owner's wealth, status and lifestyle. Finally, there were also scholars who regarded them as a moral symbol as in expressions such as "Ancient superior men found the likeness of all excellent qualities in jades." What is more, jades have also acquired some political significance as they had been used for making imperial seals and official belts.

Actually all beautiful stones are jade in the eyes of the ancients. This is also why we have such an ancient saying: "Jade is nothing but a beautiful stone."

Maid of Honour in the Shade of Tung Tree (Qing Dynasty).

Pig-head and dragon-shaped jade plate (Neolithic Age).

Jade bracelet (Neolithic Age).

Jade ruyi (Qing Dynasty).

Modern scientific experiments have shown that jade consists of two categories: hard jade and soft jade. The hard category refers specifically to jadeite while the soft jade is made mainly of a mineral element called tremolite. In China, reputable soft jade brands include Hetian Jade of Xinjiang, Lantian Jade of Shaanxi Province, Mi Jade and Du or Nanyang Jade of Henan Province, and Youyan or Xinshan Jade of Liaoning Province.

Development of Jades

Jades have been in use in China for at least 7,000-8,000 years, which can be divided into five major periods.

In the first period jade objects appeared and experienced the initial development between 8,000 and 4,000 years ago, corresponding to the Neolithic Period. By the late Neolithic

Jade dragon (Neolithic Age).

Period, China's jade objects had already developed to a relatively mature level. Examples include the C-shaped jade dragon unearthed at the site of Hongshan Culture in Northeast China and the "beast-face" jade article found at the site of Liangzhu Culture in East China. They are both jade treasures manufactured with superb skills.

The second period lasted from the late Neolithic Age to the Western Zhou Dynasty. The Erlitou Culture belonged to the late Neolithic Age during which jade weapons came into existence. Jade-making technologies improved significantly in the Shang Dynasty. In particular, during the late period of the dynasty, the variety of jade objects increased considerably compared with the first period. Jade was used for making ritual vessels, weapons, tools and daily utensils. For example, found at the ruins of Sanxingdui dating back to the late Shang Dynasty

Jade qi, a type of jade axe. (Shang Dynasty).

Jade ritual vessels: Zong (Liangzhu Culture).

were large jade articles such as a one-metre-long jade *zhang* (a type of elongated pointed jade tablet held in the hands by ancient rulers on ceremonial occasions), a round jade *bi* (a disc with a round perforation in its centre) with a diameter of 80-plus cm, some jade *huang* (an arc-shaped plaque) and jade hairpins.

The third period refers to the Spring and Autumn and Warring States Periods. The appearance of ironware during the Warring States Period led to an epochal technical advance in the making of jade objects. In shape, the traditional C-shaped jade dragon gave way to the bow-shaped one. In style, the jade articles made during this period look more vivid and realistic such as jade horses, jade birds and jade figures. Other typical jade articles include the 300-plus jade objects unearthed from the mausoleum of Marquis Yi of Zeng.

Jade dancing girl (Warring States Period).

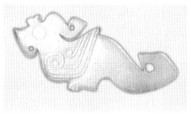

Carving of boy
(Song Dynasty).

Jade phoenix
(Shang Dynasty).

Flying deity
(Tang Dynasty).

The fourth period lasted from the Han Dynasty to the Ming Dynasty. During the Han Dynasty, with the decline in rites and rituals, the purposes of jade making shifted from serving ritual ceremonies to functioning as decorations. As a result, there appeared a large number of decorative jade articles, such as jade belt buckles, slit jade rings, jade bracelets, jade rings, jade plates as well as a multitude of animal-shaped jade ornaments. In addition, jade shrouds and other burial jade articles were also made. Hence a new height was reached in jade making.

There was a transitional stage in this period, extending from the Wei-Jin Dynasties through the Tang Dynasty. Fascinated with gold and silverware, people started to show less interest in jade articles.

By the Song Dynasty, due to the rise of archaeology, jades gradually recaptured public attention. Special markets and shops sold jade articles.

The fifth period lasted from the mid-Ming Dynasty to the Qing Dynasty. This marked the high point of Chinese jade making.

In the middle and late periods of the Ming Dynasty independent jade-making styles appeared in the hands of some highly-skilled craftsmen, paving the way technically for the continued flourish of jade art in the Qing Dynasty.

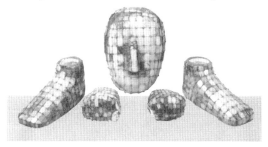

Parts of gold-lined jade shroud
(Han Dynasty).

Representing the peak of jade art in the Qing Dynasty, the imperial court jade craftsmen inherited the previous jade-making art; at the same time, they absorbed painting techniques and foreign carving styles, evolving an array of rich and exquisite skills. The best-known jade artwork is "Emperor Yu taming the river". This period also produced the first Chinese emperor passionate about collecting jades. He was none other than Emperor Qianlong. Twenty-five imperial seals were made in the Qing Dynasty and 23 of them were made of jade. Emperor Qianlong wrote some 830 poems or essays singing praises of the beauty and purity of jades and expounding his aesthetic views on jade artworks.

A number of literary works also appeared whose characters respected and loved jades, and could not tear themselves away from them. The best-known example was Cao Xueqin's *Dream of Red Chamber*. A precious jadestone functioned like a thread that linked the rise and fall of noble houses and the love story between the hero and the heroine.

Emperor Yu taming
the river
(Qing Dynasty).

Gold-Lined Jade Shroud

During the Han Dynasty, people believed that jades could preserve the bodies and jade shrouds were thus woven for the deceased so

that their bodies could stay intact forever. Such shrouds are of course only affordable to emperors and princes. These emperors or princes were covered by armour-like jade shrouds made up of numerous jade plates that were sewn together with gold threads. The ritual institutions of the Han Dynasty stipulated that such shrouds had three categories in the thread used: gold thread for emperors; silver thread for princes; and copper thread for emperors' concubines and sisters. Yet most princes then chose gold threads, a fact indicating their disregard for the emperor. A jade shroud consisted of five parts: helmet, jacket, trousers, gloves and shoes. There were eye-covering, nose plugs, ear plugs and mouth plugs in the helmet. In the lower-abdominal area was a small box covering the sex organ and an anus plug.

Classification of Jades

Jade articles fall into four major categories based on their functions.

First, ritual jades. These were used in ritual ceremonies like offering sacrifice to deities and ancestors, tribute paying, military operations and diplomatic activities. According to the *Record of Rites*, ritual jades consisted of "six objects" and "six tallies". The six objects were *bi* (disc), *cong* (tubes with a square cross-section and a circular hole), *gui*, *zhang*, *huang* and *hu* (tiger jade). They were used in the rite of offering sacrifice to heaven and earth as well as deities, forming the core of ancient Chinese ritual jades. The six tallies referred to four types of *gui* and two types of *bi*, which were worn by princes, dukes, marquises, counts, viscounts and barons as emblems of their noble status and identities.

Bi.   Huang.   Cong.

Bi is a flat jade disc with a round perforation in its centre that first appeared in the Neolithic Period. It is the earliest and also the most enduring jade article used in the ceremony of offering sacrifice to heaven. It was also a nice souvenir that can be worn as an ornament, as well as a burial item.

Huang is a semi-circular ritual jade object featuring complicated patterns. It is found in huge quantities and has enjoyed the longest popularity. It was used in offering sacrifice to the north. A legend has it that it was created by the ancients in imitation of the rainbow in the sky after rain.

Cong is a tube-shaped jade article with a square cross-section and a circular hole. It first emerged in the Neolithic Period and prevailed in the period of Liangzhu Culture. Scholars speculated that the jade's square and circle represented heaven and earth and it was mainly used in heaven-worshipping practices. It is also argued that it is a symbol of wealth and power. Another contention was that it signified the female and reflects the ancient worship of the sex organ.

Second, jade tools which first appeared in the Neolithic and Bronze Ages. With the advent of bronze and iron articles, jade tools went into oblivion gradually. A fundamental reason was that jade tools were hard but brittle. Typical jade tools include jade axe, dagger, chisel, heavy ring and dagger-axe.

Third, jade utensils that first appeared in the Shang Dynasty such as jade *gui* (a round-mouthed food vessel with two or four loop handles). Later, there also emerged jade incense burners, jade goblets, jade lanterns, jade bowls, jade wine vessels, jade combs and jade hairpins as well as jade treasures of the study.

Fourth, decorative jades including mainly jade screens, jade animals, jade mountains, jade *ruyi*, jade *jue* (slit rings), jade *huang* and jade bangles.

Jade mountains: Jade-carved mountains with trees, houses and figures on them. Garden and landscape were the dominant themes.

Jade *huang*: As one of the earliest jade ornaments, it appeared in the Neolithic Period. It is generally deemed to be related to the dragon. This can be inferred from the expression — "*sui shen dai long* (having the dragon about all the time)". Here the dragon refers actually to the arc-shaped *huang*. Later it developed into a ritual article.

Jade axe (Neolithic Age).

Jade dagger (Neolithic Age).

Jade inkstone
(Qing Dynasty).

Jade cup
(Qin Dynasty).

Jade comb
(Warring States Period).

Jade *jue*: This appeared in the Neolithic Period as the mother of earrings.
Jade *ruyi*: As an emblem of peace and prosperity, it was usually given out as gifts. It was believed to be the first gift ever given by the Chinese emperor to the English King.

Jade Mountain: "Lao Zi leaving the Hangu pass". Trees, cottages and persons are carved on it. This type of jade artwork focuses thematically on gardens and landscape (Qing Dynasty).

Jade screen: Refining the pills of immortality (Qing Dynasty).

Jade ruyi (Qing Dynasty): As a symbol of peace and prosperity, it was usually given out as gifts. It is said that the first gift given by the Chinese emperor to the English king was a jade ruyi.

Jade jue (slit ring): Called the forefather of earrings, it first appeared in the Neolithic Age.

A legend has it that the Heshi Jade mentioned in the story of "*wan bi gui zhao*" (The Jade Returned to the State of Zhao Intact) was later used by the first emperor of the Qin Dynasty for carving an imperial seal. The emperor hoped that the precious stone would bring eternity to his dynasty. The seal was inherited by emperors of subsequent dynasties for some 1,500 years until the fall of the Ming Dynasty. The seal was taken by the Mongols to the northern desert area and disappeared forever from Chinese history.

The Making of Jades

Jade making goes through four stages: choosing, painting, grinding and polishing.

Choosing: The jade quality is analyzed and studied for the final choice. Colour, hardness, texture and shape are the major factors that need to be considered in designing.

Painting: The designed patterns are painted on the chosen stone.

Grinding: This refers to the process in which the jade is ground with specially-designed iron tools such as synthetic emery and natural garnet.

Polishing: There are two polishing methods. First, for naked jade objects like jade bangles, jade buttons and jade hearts, manual polishing is required by means of sandpaper. The other method is mechanical polishing which uses polishing cream or powder. Sometimes, these two methods need to be combined in order to weave a glossy and smart "coat" for the end products.

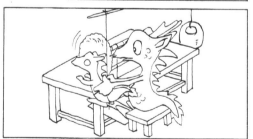

Jade Storage

1. Avoid knocking, dropping and burning.

   Storing jades is an easy matter. Yet tough as they are, they are very brittle. They will crack or break easily when knocked or burned.

2. Don't put them in a humid environment for a long time. Keep them away from saline, acidic and alkaline substances. Generally, jade articles are not affected by extreme temperatures and high humidity. However, if they are stored in a humid condition for long, cracks may appear on their surfaces. Therefore, it is important to keep them in a dry, clean and well-ventilated place. The best method is to get a special wooden box in which are placed desiccant, sponge, cotton and other moisture-absorbing soft materials.

How to Make your Jades Look Brighter

1. Put the jade article into a basin together with an appropriate amount of caustic soda, and pour in some hot water slowly. Keep it there for half a day.

2. In case of stains found on the jade article, you may brush it repeatedly and wash it with clean water.

3. Wipe off the water drops with towel; let it dry before scattering some white wax powder on it.

4. Put the jade into an oven and heat it gradually. (Don't start at high temperature as that will cause the jade to crack.)

5. Take the jade out of the oven when the wax powder melts. Brush the jade evenly so that the wax goes into the jade surface.

6. Remove the wax remains with a soft hair brush; brush it with a hard brush repeatedly until gloss emerge; and polish it with a towel. Now we get a jade that looks brighter.

Jade Authentication

The ancients laid down five criteria in authenticating jade articles: warm, moist and glossy; uniform veins both inside and outside; clear and clarion sounds; hard and dense; and clean and pure in colour. Modern authenticators follow five.

1. Jade Texture

Smoothness and fineness come first in jade authentication. This is what sets jades apart fundamentally from common stones. The smoother and finer the jade, the purer it is.

2. Jade Hardness

Hardness is also an important criterion. This can be measured by scratching or cutting. Without a hardness meter, we may use some substitutes for reference. For example, one degree of hardness applies when the surface can be scratched with a piece of paper; 2.5 degrees corresponds to that of our nails; 3.5 degrees equals that of copper; 5.5-6 degrees, glass; and 6-7 degrees, steel knife.

3. Transparency

The transparency is proportionate to texture. The higher transparency, the smoother and finer. A high transparency can also enhance the colour. There are four degrees for measuring transparency:

3.1: Transparent: amber, brown quartz and crystals;

3.2 Subtransparent: agate and rose quartz;

3.3: Translucent: jade and emerald;

3.4: Opaque: malachite and turquoise.

4. Specific Gravity of Jade

Jade's specific gravity ranges between 2 and 3. Frequently-used methods for measuring its specific gravity include balance method, pycnometer method and the method of specific gravity solution.

5. Jade Colours

Colours of jade result from its mineral elements. For example, jade green is caused by the content of chrome while pea green and deep green are attributable to iron oxide. For common jadeite, pure jade green is important, and its price is related incrementally to its degree of density, purity, evenness and regularity. For white jade, top quality means tallow white.

A Multitude of Chinese Characters Related to Jade

"Five thousand years of history, / Is linked up by jade." The Chinese people respect, love, appreciate and wear jade objects. There are some 500 Chinese characters connected directly or indirectly with jade. There are also about 100 Chinese idioms related to the precious stone. As for phrases in this regard, the number is uncountable.

Chinese character with the radical of "*yu*玉 (actually 王)"

玕(gan, pearly stone) 玖 (jiu, dark-hued jade-like stone) 珏 (jue, slit jade ring) 琪 (qi, fine jade) 瑶 (yao, precious jade) 球 (qiu, fine jade) 璞 (pu, uncut jade) 琨 (kun, beautiful jade) 琼 (qiong, red jade) 琅 (lang, pearl-like stone) 琳 (lin, beautiful jade) 环 (huan, jade ring) 璜 (huang, semi-circular jade pendant) ……

Chinese idioms:
冰肌玉骨　(bing ji yu gu, white as ice and smooth as jade)
冰清玉洁　(bing qing yu jie, pure like jade and clear like ice)
璞玉浑金　(pu yu hun jin, uncarved jade and unrefined gold; unadorned beauty)
不吝金玉　(bu lin jin yu, do not grudge gold and jade (material pursuit))
金科玉律　(jin ke yu lu, the golden rule)
金石为开　(jin shi wei kai, good faith can break gold and jade)
金玉满堂　(jin yu man tang, one's house is filled with gold, jade and other treasures)
金玉良言　(jin yu liang yan, honest advice which is as important as gold and jade)
锦衣玉食 (jin yi yu shi, silk dress and jade-like food; living an extravagant life)
美如冠玉　(mei ru guan yu, having a beautiful jade hat; a handsome man)
亭亭玉立　(ting ting yu li, slim and graceful)
金枝玉叶　(jin zhi yu ye, golden bough and jade leaves; imperial kinsmen)
抛砖引玉　(pao zhuan yin yu, throw out a brick to attract a jade; give some introductory remarks that may elicit valuable opinions)
珠圆玉润　(zhu yuan yu run, round as pearls and smooth as jade; golden throat or excellent writing style)

The Jade is Returned to the State of Zhao Intact

During the Warring States Period, Lord Zhao of Qin heard that the treasured Heshi Jade was in the hands of Lord Hui of Zhao. So he sent an envoy to Zhao.

Qin wants to exchange Heshi Jade with 15 cities.

What shall I do if I agree but Qin refuses to hand over the promised cities?

Your Highness, Qin is stronger than us. You cannot say no.

Your Highness, please allow me, Lin Xiangru, to visit Qin with the jade. I won't disappoint you.

Good. I can entrust the task to you.

What a beautiful jade!

Extraordinary indeed!

Something is amiss!

The lord of Qin does not want to talk about the 15 cities!

Your Highness, the jade is matchless in this world.

But still it has defects. Let me show you.

No! No! No!

Get me a map and I will cross 15 cities for the State of Zhao!

Your Highness, the lord of Zhao took a bath and fasted for five days before I left for Qin with the jade.

Therefore, I would like Your Highness to receive the jade with the same rituals in order to show your sincerity.

Lin Xiangru sent the jade back to the State of Zhao by a path...

...while the lord of Qin was fasting.

Five days later...

Your Highness, Qin has over 20 lords since Lord Mu and few of them honour their promises.

I'm very upset, but your courage is respectable. I should send you back to Zhao.

Later, "*wan bi gui zhao* (the jade is returned to Zhao intact)" became an idiom to describe anything that is returned intact.

So I have sent the jade back to Zhao.

If Your Highness does want to exchange your cities for the jade, please hand over the cities to the lord of Zhao first.

Then my lord will surely present the jade to you as agreed.

Nongyu Plays the Flute

When the daughter of Lord Mu of Qin was born, somebody gave the family a piece of green jade. During the traditional ceremony in which the child's future ambition was determined by what he/she picked out of the various symbolic objects laid on a table, the daughter chose the jade and held it firmly in her hand.

Since you like to play with this jade, I will name you "Nongyu".

When Nongyu grew up, she liked to play the bamboo flute. So Lord Mu had the green jade fashioned into a flute for her.

What sweet melody my daughter plays with her flute!

A young man named Xiao Shi also liked to play the flute very much. He could imitate how the male and female phoenixes sang in harmony.

Nongyu, you look worried these days. Are you thinking of that flute player?

Yes.

So Lord Mu married Nongyu to Xiao Shi and constructed them a platform of phoenixes.

Xiao Shi taught Nongyu to play the sound of male and female phoenixes singing together.

One day, Xiao Shi and Nongyu rode on a dragon and a phoenix and flew to the sky.

Queen of the State of Qi Unjoins the Linking Rings

During the Warring States Period, the first emperor of Qin sent a set of jade linking rings to the queen of the State of Qi.

The Qi people are resourceful. Let me see if they can untie the rings.

Take a look and see if they can be untied.

Your Highness, we cannot untie these linked rings.

Really?

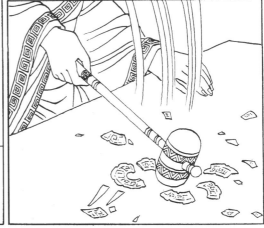

Well, there you are.

It seems that the State of Qi would rather be a broken jade than a brick intact.

It's not the right time to attack Qi.

LACQUERWARE

Lacquerware is an ancient and highly valuable art. It has a 7,000-year-old history. The lacquer coating is made of the sap from the lacquer tree and mixed with other dyes. Lacquerware has a smooth and shiny surface. Drawings and patterns are painted on them to form an eye-catching piece of art. As lacquer has been glazed on the surface, lacquerware is thus very durable.

In the Tang Dynasty, lacquer carving created a milestone for lacquerware. Lacquer carving involves painting layer after layer of lacquer on a brass or wooden body. Before the layer dries, patterns like humans, floral and fauna, landscape, dragon and phoenix were carved on the lacquer coating.

Usually, lacquer carving uses the vermilion lacquer. There are many kinds of items which use lacquer carving. They include tables, chairs, cabinets, shelves as well as stationery items.

BRONZES

*Eye-protruding mask
(Late Shang Dynasty).*

*Ban gui (food vessel)
(Warring States Period).*

Bronzes are representative of Chinese culture. They are a great human invention achieved thousands of years ago. They are the pride of Chinese people. Thanks to their unique shapes, exquisite designs and elegant inscriptions based on the casting technologies and cultural advancements in the pre-Qin period, they are regarded by historians as a living book of history.

*Bronze galloping steed
(Eastern Han Dynasty).*

What are Bronzes?

Bronze refers to an alloy of copper, tin, nickel, lead, phosphorus and other elements. In ancient times it was called "gold" or "propitious gold". The bronze objects, which were buried underground for thousands of years, acquired a layer of dark green rust as a result of oxidation. That was why archaeologists named these objects "propitious gold" or "*qing tong qi*" (literally dark-green objects or simply bronzes)".

*Bronze dui
(Warring States Period).*

Development of bronzes in China

The Bronze Age of China mainly refers to the Shang Dynasty and the Western and Eastern Zhou Dynasties. Chinese bronzes underwent three stages in development:

First, the stage of formation in the Neolithic Period or 4,500 to 4,000 years ago. The number of bronze objects cast during this period was quite small and most of them were daily tools and utensils. Besides bronzes, brass and copper objects also appeared.

Second, the stage of flourishing development lasting for more than 1,600 years from the Xia Dynasty through the early Warring States Period. This was the Bronze Age in Chinese history. Bronze objects manufactured in this period consisted mainly of musical instruments, weapons and miscellaneous articles. Designs and patterns inscribed were beast faces, cicadas and other ferocious creatures. Jade, gold and silver were also inlaid in some bronze objects.

Thitd, the transitional stage in which ritual bronze vessels gave way to everyday utensils such as bronze mirrors and lamps. Bronze weapons were replaced by iron weapons. This transition took place in a period covering the late Warring States Period, the Qin Dynasty and the Western Han Dynasty. In a sense, bronzes entered a period of decline.

Flat-bottomed jue (wine vessel) (Xia Dynasty).

Dayu cauldron (Western Zhou Dynasty).

Boshan incense burner (Western Han Dynasty).

Features of Chinese Bronzes

Like bronzes discovered in other parts of the world, Chinese bronzes feature high hardness, convenience for long-term collection, antique and elegant appearance and multiple shapes. At the same time, they also stand out with four distinct attractions:

First, large in number and great in variety. China has unearthed countless bronze objects of many categories. In addition to wine vessels, water and food vessels and weapons, there were also many types of tools and miscellaneous implements.

Tea table (Warring States).

Second, wide distribution and high quality. Bronzes can be found all over China. The unique and precise alloy compositions guarantee their exceptional quality.

Third, Chinese bronzes set themselves apart with their inscriptions rarely found in the bronzes unearthed elsewhere in the world. Compared with the small number of Indian inscribed bronzes, most Chinese bronzes have inscriptions, some of which run very long.

Circular Mengjiang hu vessel (Spring and Autumn Period).

Fourth, vessels are the dominant bronze objects in Chinese history while bronze weapons prevail elsewhere. A case in point is *ding* or cauldron which evolved gradually from its original function as a vessel into a symbol of state power.

A bronze cauldron with kui legs (Shang Dynasty).

A big nao with
beast-face designs
(Shang Dynasty).

A shi hu vessel with cloud-
and-thunder designs
(Shang Dynasty).

A military cauldron
with bird designs
(Western Zhou Dynasty).

Designs and Inscriptions on Bronzes

The designs on bronzes added to their ferocious beauty. These designs were mainly based on animals while others were geometric or curvaceous.

The earliest bronze designs were based on distorted patterns, such as beast faces, dragons, banana leaves, clouds and lightning. On top of delicate designs, Chinese bronzes were also inscribed with characters. These were called "bronze inscriptions".

In the late Shang Dynasty, events were recorded in bronze inscriptions. By the rise of the Zhou Dynasty, people started to inscribe their achievements and honours on bronzes. This was done in the hope of propitiating their forefathers and immortalising their deeds in the minds of their descendants.

The Mao Gong *ding* (cauldron) was cast by Duke Mao to extend his acknowledgement and tribute to the emperor of the Zhou Dynasty during the late Western Zhou period. Among all extant ancient bronzes, this *ding* has the longest inscription of 479 Chinese characters.

A bronze ritual vessel cast before 900 BC
with a 284-character bronze inscription,
recording some state affairs and ancestral
achievements during the reigns of
Emperor Wen and five other emperors.

Words on Mao
Gong ding.

Mao Gong ding.

Classification of Chinese Bronzes

Bronzes were indispensable to the ancient Chinese in their ritual practices such as offering sacrifice to deities and ancestors, and praying for favourable weather. That was also why some of them were known as "ritual vessels". Based on their differing uses, Chinese bronzes can be divided into food vessels, wine vessels, musical instruments, weapons, farming implements and miscellaneous articles.

1. Food Vessels

Common bronzes include *ding*, *dou*, *gui*, *zeng*, *li*, *pan* and *dui*.

Ding was a cauldron-like vessel used for cooking or storing meat. It may be three-legged or four-legged; it may or may not have a lid. It was the most enduring bronze object, and also the commonest and most mysterious "ritual vessel". Later as time went by, its original function as food vessels was reduced and its symbolic function as an emblem of state power was highlighted.

Simuwu rectangular *ding* is the largest and also the heaviest bronze object unearthed so far. It is the king in the realm of *ding*. It is 875 kg in weight, 133 cm in height and 110 cm in length.

It was cast by Emperor Wen of the Shang Dynasty in memory of his mother.

Dou is a small vessel designed specially for storing pickles, minced meat and sauces.

Dou with the hunting design (Spring and Autumn Period).

Gui is a large bowl-like food vessel.

Li Gui vessel (Western Zhou Dynasty) was the earliest bronzeware made in the said dynasty unearthed so far.

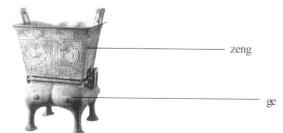

— zeng

— ge

Yan (Spring and Autumn Period).

Marquis Wu of Chen's Dui (Warring States Period).

San Shi Pan (Western Zhou Dynasty): 19 lines of inscriptions were found on the interior of its stomach, adding up to a 357-character contract.

Heavenly Gu.

Dragon Jue.

Yan is a steamer. The upper part for holding the food is called *zeng* while the lower part for holding water is termed *ge*. *Ge* is also used for cooking porridge.

Dui looks very much like *gui* in function. Also used for holding food, it usually comes with a lid.

Pan is a water vessel. Bronze *pan* appeared in the early Shang Dynasty and became popular during the late part of the dynasty. Guo Ji Zi *pan* is the biggest unearthed thus far. This big *pan*, San Shi *pan* and Mao **Gong *ding*** are collectively called the "Three Major Bronze Vessels of the Western Zhou Dynasty".

Dui is used for storing food made from millet, rice and sorghum.

2. Wine Vessels

A Chinese saying says that "rituals cannot be established without wine". Bronze wine vessels are an integral part of ancient China's ritual vessels. Bronze vessels like *jue*, *gu*, *zhi*, *jia* and *gong* can be used for pouring and drinking wine. Bronze vessels for holding wine include mainly *zun*, *you*, *fang yi*, *lei* and *he*.

Jue, which appeared in the Xia Dynasty, is China's earliest bronze ritual vessel. *Jue* and **gu** form a simple pair of wine vessels. Heavenly *gu* and dragon *jue* are both wine vessels used in the early Western Zhou period. A Chinese idiom reads, "One cannot use *gu* randomly for drinking," implying that the number of *gu* one has is related to one's status, integrity and drinking capacity. Only a high-ranking man was entitled to use this type of wine vessel.

Zun and **you** are both exalted wine vessels. The phrase "*zun gui*" (honourable, respected) is said to originate from this vessel. The square *Zun* with four sheep was cast in the late Shang Dynasty. It is the largest *zun* so far discovered in China. Four sheep facing four dragons are carved on the vessel, a perfect embodiment of the noble spirit possessed by this wine vessel.

| *Bronze zhi.* | *Gong.* | *Jia.* | *Square yi.* |

3. Musical Instruments

Many kinds of bronze musical instruments have been unearthed in China. The earliest were bronze bells. Bronze bells with petal patterns were cast in the late Shang Dynasty. The original bell was 12.15 cm in height, and its clapper 10.3 cm long. Shaped like a trumpet, it has an upper hold, four petals and a clapper hanging inside. Other bronze musical instruments included *nao, zheng, bo* and *chun. Bian zhong* or a chime of bells, which prevailed during the Spring and Autumn Period, were a very important type of ancient Chinese musical instruments. Placed on a wooden rack from the smaller to the bigger, these bronze bells are capable of producing clear and penetrating sounds. The best known set of bells was unearthed from the mausoleum of Marquis Yi of Zeng who had them cast about 2,400 years ago. They are the largest chime of bells ever discovered in China, and they can produce a wide range of sounds in a grand style. They are famed as the "King of Bronze Bells".

A chime of bronze bells unearthed from the tomb of Marquis Yi of Zeng (Warring States Period).

A bronze bell with petal patterns (Zhou Dynasty).

Bronze nao (Zhou Dynasty).

4. Weapons

"The major state affairs consist of offering sacrifices to deities and ancestors, and in waging wars." Bronze ritual vessels and weapons appeared almost simultaneously in the Xia Dynasty. Bronze weapons include battle-axe, dagger, sword, dagger-axe, lance and halberd.

Dagger-axe: As one of the unique Chinese bronze weapons, it was widely used during the Shang and Zhou Dynasties. It evolved out of farming tools.

Lance: A thrusting weapon that prevailed during the Western Zhou Dynasty and the Spring and Autumn Period.

Halberd: A highly effective weapon made by mounting the dagger-axe on the upper end of the lance, it was capable of thrusting and hooking.

Battleaxe: This was the commonest weapon used for cutting.

Sword: Often used for defending oneself, and also for stabbing and chopping. During the Han Dynasty, iron swords became popular and took the place of bronze ones.

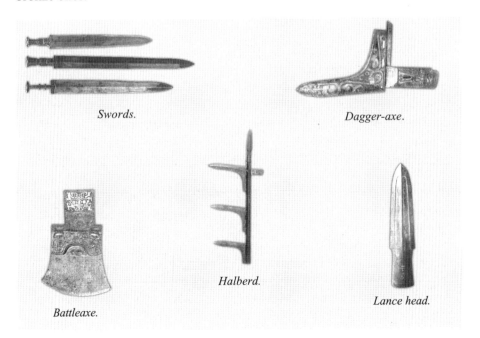

Swords.

Dagger-axe.

Halberd.

Lance head.

Battleaxe.

5. Farming Implements

Major bronze farming tools are shovels and adzes for reclaiming land.

6. Miscellaneous Bronzes

Besides the above major categories, there were also other bronze objects for daily domestic use. Bronze mirrors originated from the Qijia Culture which existed in China 4,000 years ago. Bronze mirrors made at that time were very rough in quality. By the Warring States Period and the Western and Eastern Han Dynasties, mirror-making technologies improved significantly. People also started to cast all kinds of designs and patterns on mirrors.

Other daily bronze objects included incense burners, staff heads, bronze coins, combs, figures and facial masks.

Bronze boxes (Warring States Period).

Liushan bronze mirror (Western Han Dynasty).

Bird-shaped bronze staff (Spring and Autumn Period).

Qin bronzes unearthed at Lintong, Shaanxi Province

More than 10,000 pieces of bronze weapons were discovered at the site of the Qin Emperor's terra-cotta warriors and horses in Xi'an, ranging from swords to dagger-axes and lances. Buried underground for over 2,000 years, some of them are still very sharp. The well-known bronze chariots and horses constitute the largest, the most vividly decorated and also the best rigged ancient Chinese bronze artefacts. Each chariot is drawn by four horses and operated by a terra-cotta driver. The two bronze chariots are made of some 7,000 parts and components, testifying to the advanced bronze-

making technologies of China during the Qin Dynasty. These chariots and horses are hailed as the "Champion of Chinese Bronzes".

"The First Lamp of China"or the Changxin Palace Lantern. As a lighting device, it was once used in the Changxin Palace for Queen Dou of the Western Han Dynasty. A result of high craft, this lantern is made in such a style that aspires towards freedom, ease and elegance in shaping and decoration, a clear departure from the previous style stressing mystery and massiveness. In a word, it is a rare lighting device that fuses practical and aesthetic properties.

The Ruins of Sanxingdui

The ruins located in Guanghan of Sichuan Province amazed the world with its grand scale.

Found there were bronze standing figures which look rather exaggerated with over-long arms, eyes sticking out like columns, big ears and other non-Asian facial features.

Eye-protruding mask (Shang Dynasty).

Eye-protruding masks were cast in the late Shang Dynasty. They are the largest and also the earliest bronze masks found so far across the world. Shaped in a simple yet odd style, these masks look enigmatic.

Erect figures were cast in the late Shang Dynasty with a height of 172 cm, standing on a 90-cm-high pedestal. Encapsulating the features of deities, witches and kings, these figures are the tallest bronze figures ever found. They are called the "King of the World Bronze Figures".

Sacred tree (Shang Dynasty).

Standing figure (Shang Dynasty).

Bronze sacred trees: There are sacred birds on these trees. Each tree, 384 cm high, has three clumps of branches featuring 27 fruits and nine birds.

Authentication of Bronzes

Fake bronzes date back to the Song Dynasty. The classical-minded scholar-officials then reproduced a fair number of bronzes with kind intentions. However, in the Republic Period (1911–1949) as well as over the past two decades, profit-driven forgery has gone rampant. To authenticate a bronze work, one needs to pay close attention to rust colour, feel, sound, designs and patterns, and bronze texture.

1. Rust colours. Different textures result in different rust colours. Common colours are green patina, red rust, blue rust, dark rust and purple rust. If the rust colours glare and stink, and taste salty, it must be fake rust.

2. Feel. One may feel the bronze and be cautious if it is too light or too heavy.

3. Sound. If you knock an authentic bronze, it should produce a light and clear sound. Otherwise, it must be a fake.

4. Designs and patterns. One needs to know well the designs and patterns on bronze objects of different historical periods. Early bronzes have simple and plain designs while later bronzes feature complex ones.

5. Bronze texture. Turn over the bronze object. If copper colour is detected, it should be fakes. If the underside is also forged, a combination of the above methods is required for an overall analysis in conjunction with one's understanding of the characteristics of each dynasty's bronzeware.

How did the Ancients Make Bronzes?

First step: preparing materials (copper ore sand) and tools (bronze-making crucible).

Second step: selecting fine copper ore.

Third step: initial smelting. Put the selected ore and charcoal into the crucible and light it. The ore turns into molten copper through burning. This is the so-called coarse copper.

Fourth step: refining and adding tin. Refine the coarse copper further and add in varying amounts of tin depending on what objects one wants to make.

Fifth step: casting bronze.

First, make a mould for the intended bronze object; paint designs and patterns on it with a red writing brush; make a depression where needed and attach a piece of clay where a projection is desired. (Later, wax moulds were also used.)	Second, reproduce the designs and inscriptions. Mix the clay evenly and put it on the mould and press it hard so that the mould's designs and inscriptions are reproduced onto the clay. When the clay is half dry, process it into an external model and an internal one.	The internal model is smaller than the external one, and molten bronze is poured in between after they are joined up. Third, grind. When the molten bronze hardens, take out the object and grind it slightly. At last a perfect bronze object is made.

Gan Jiang and Mo Ye

You have grown up, let me tell you, Chibi.

Your father Gan Jiang was a well-known swordsmith.

Mother, where's my father?

Over 10 years ago, the lord of Chu ordered your father to cast swords. It took us three years to cast a pair of swords. The *yang* sword was named after your father Gan Jiang, the *yin* one after me.

Your father knew the lord wanted to have both swords and then kill the smith. So he went to see the lord with only the *yang* sword.

After I go, you must get away from here and take good care of our son. When our son grows up, tell him to look out of the door at the Southern Mountain.

The other sword is hidden behind the pine growing on a stone.

Your father never returned. The lord killed him.

Grr...

Don't worry! I won't let you down.

Swish!

Your Highness, I have got the boy's head.

Ha! Ha! Give our hero a thousand gold coins!

You cannot hurt me any longer!

Your Highness, that's a hero's head. You should boil it in a cauldron so that his ghost won't bother you any more.

You're right. I will boil it!

The lord is killed!

Don't let the assassin run away!

Catch him!

Ha! Ha!

Ah! The three heads are all deformed. We cannot tell which is our lord's and which are the others.

So they divided the three heads evenly into three parts and buried them separately southwest of today's Runan County, Henan Province, in accordance with the lordly rituals. The three tombs have been known as "the Lord's Three Tombs".

Inquiring about the Cauldrons in the Central Plains

Nine cauldrons were cast with bronze presented by nine vassal states when Emperor Yu worked hard to tame the flooding river. They were symbols of the nine vassal states as well as the state power. During the Xia, Shang and Zhou Dynasties, they were viewed as national treasures that were handed down from one generation to another.

In the closing years of the Zhou Dynasty, the State of Chu became a power. Its army defeated the Quanrong forces in Luhun.

Lord Zhuang conducted a military review at the border of the Zhou territory to show off his military might.

I'm like an extraordinary bird. It does not fly unless it touches the sky. It does not cry unless it amazes the world with a loud, clear voice.

King Ding of Zhou became upset and dispatched Minister Wang Sunman to extend his regards to the Chu army.

Go and see what they want to do after all.

I am told that the nine cauldrons cast by King Yu are considered national treasures in Luoyang.

We also have cauldrons in the State of Chu. May I know the sizes and weights of yours?

I, Wang Sunman, am commissioned by His Majesty to come and reward the Chu army.

Ha! Ha! You have come at the right time!

What the great Zhou Dynasty stresses is virtue instead of cauldrons.

With virtue, a small cauldron becomes heavy; without virtue, a huge cauldron will become light.

The Xia Dynasty founded by King Yu ruled by virtue. That is why the vassal lords presented Xia with bronze. Nine cauldrons were cast to represent the nine vassal states and protect the subjects from demons and monsters.

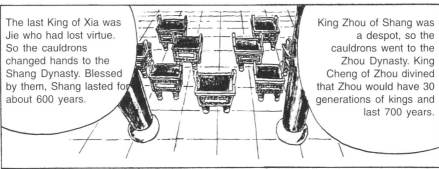

The last King of Xia was Jie who had lost virtue. So the cauldrons changed hands to the Shang Dynasty. Blessed by them, Shang lasted for about 600 years.

King Zhou of Shang was a despot, so the cauldrons went to the Zhou Dynasty. King Cheng of Zhou divined that Zhou would have 30 generations of kings and last 700 years.

The virtue of Zhou have declined, but the Mandate of Heaven cannot be violated. It is improper for you to ask about the weights of the cauldrons.

Well, I will stop here. With a tiny part of the scrap iron in the storehouse of Chu we can cast nine cauldrons.

After that, Lord Zhuang of Chu started to take virtue seriously in handling affairs and eventually became an overlord.

Invention of the Bronze Mirror

A long time ago, there was no mirror. The only way a person could take a look at himself was to look at his reflection in the river.

Later, people stored water in a big basin at home for that purpose.

Much later, people used a bronzeware with a concave centre to start a fire by placing it under the sun.

This round bronzeware with a concave centre will generate high heat as the heat from the sun is concentrated on a particular spot. Placing flammable items on that spot will start a fire.

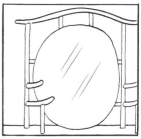

By chance, they discovered that the bronzeware was reflective.

Inspired, the bronzeware was flattened to become a mirror.

This was how the first bronze mirror came about.

Son of Heaven Mirror

In the past, a bronze mirror was a very valuable item. It could even be used as an article of tribute to the emperor.

During the Tang Dynasty, artisans in Yangzhou got together to make exquisite bronze mirrors during the Dumpling Festival to be given as articles of tribute to the court. This type of mirror was called Son of Heaven Mirror. On Emperor Tang Minghuang's birthday on the fifth day of the eighth month in AD 730, officials of the fourth grade and above were each bestowed a bronze mirror. This day was later designated as the Thousand Autumn Golden Sign Festival. Anyone who did not belong to the royal family had to present a bronze mirror. Soon, this custom was practised among the commoners who gave one another bronze mirrors on this day.

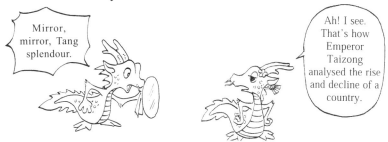

Mirror, mirror, Tang splendour.

Ah! I see. That's how Emperor Taizong analysed the rise and decline of a country.

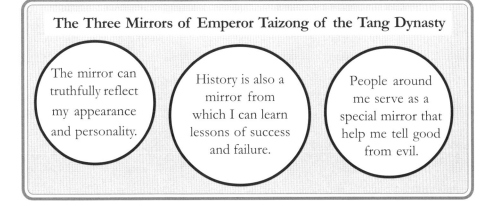

The Three Mirrors of Emperor Taizong of the Tang Dynasty

The mirror can truthfully reflect my appearance and personality.

History is also a mirror from which I can learn lessons of success and failure.

People around me serve as a special mirror that help me tell good from evil.

Much effort and care went into the making of bronze mirrors of old. It was not just a daily item; it was also a piece of art.

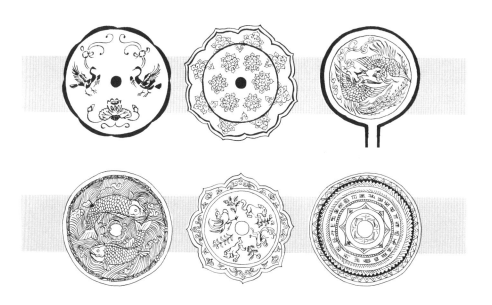

In Chinese ghost stories, demons who possessed humans would have their true forms revealed in the mirror. That was why there were frequent references to priests using the mirror to reveal a demon's true form.

Some houses also hung a mirror above their doors to ward off evil.

A bride in ancient times would also carry a small bronze mirror with her to ward off evil.

A Broken Mirror Repaired

During the Northern and Southern Dynasties, Princess Lechang of the Chen Dynasty and her husband Xu Deyan, a talent in South China, lived a happy life in their mansion. They were a perfect couple.

Soon afterwards, the Sui army occupied Jiankang (Nanjing) and the Chen Dynasty came to an end.

Princess, this bronze mirror is broken. You take one half, and I the other.

No matter what will happen, you should take good care of yourself.

If I survive this disaster, I will go and sell the broken mirror at a market in Chang'an. We'll be reunited…

Xu Deyan was right. He and his wife got separated while escaping from the war…

The princess ended up in the mansion of Yang Su, a powerful minister in the Sui Dynasty, and became the latter's beloved concubine. Holding the broken mirror in hand, she missed her husband very much, especially on moonlit nights.

Each year, on the 15th day of the first month, she would ask one of her old servants to go to the said market with the broken mirror.

The third year...

Ah! She has become the concubine of the powerful Duke Yueguo!

Xu Yande wrote a poem on the mirror and left dejected.

She and the mirror were gone together, / The mirror has returned alone. / The image of Chang'e has disappeared, / Only the moon shining there brightly.

Help! The princess has fainted!

Yang Su threw a banquet and Xu Yande was invited.

My husband has presented the other half of the bronze mirror. He is in town.

I cannot bear to let him go. Please grant us a meeting.

Princess Lechang has great talents. I will invite her to pen a verse for the guests.

What a trick of life today,
My current beau faces my ex-beau.
I dare not smile or weep,
It's hard indeed to be a woman.

Her poem moved everyody present.

Yang Su was so deeply touched that he declared promptly that he would approve their reunion and allow them to go back to their hometown. His kindness has also become a much-told story.

Xu Yande and Princess Lechang went back to southern China and lived a tranquil life.

In the tenth year during the reign of Emperor Taizong of the Tang Dynasty, the couple passed away within the same year. They were buried together with the repaired bronze mirror.

CLAY MODELLING

It is said that when the earth was first formed, there was no human life.

These clay face masks, clay figurines and clay oxen were found at ancient sites.

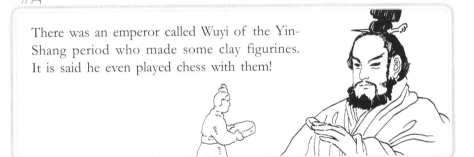

There was an emperor called Wuyi of the Yin-Shang period who made some clay figurines. It is said he even played chess with them!

Three Categories of Clay Figurines

Images of Confucius and Buddha

Buddhism spread to China during the Eastern
Han Period. Images of Buddha first appeared in
Han-Jin times and flourished during the Tang
Dynasty. They were more than just an image for
worship and gave Buddhist art a headstart.

Burial Items

In China's primitive society, slaves were
regarded as property. When the master died,
the slaves had to be buried with him. When it
came to the Western Zhou Dynasty, as
agriculture flourished, the labour of slaves
became an important source of production. And
so the old burial custom was gradually lost.
Figurines made of grass, wood or clay took the
place of human slaves in the burial custom.

Niren Zhang

The famous Niren Zhang from Tianjin is a top-rate coloured clay
modelling art-form in northern China. It has its origins in the late Qing
Dynasty. To this day, it has been passed down five generations. The
first-generation Niren Zhang, Zhang Mingshan, had been adept at
kneading clay into figurines since he was a child. It is said he would
hide some clay in his sleeves whenever he went to watch
operas. As he watched the actors, he would knead figurines
of them. Before the show ended,
he would have made vivid clay
models of the characters. Niren
Zhang has a wide repertoire that
includes character caricature,
folklore and mythical characters,
etc.

Clay Toys

Clay toys became very common in China at the start of the Tang Dynasty. It was a folk art that was suitable for both the young and the old. Even the emperor took a liking to them.

Wuxi, Hangzhou, Suzhou and Tianjin count among the more famous places for clay toys. Clay toys are not just limited to images of children. They also include opera figures, God of Longevity, top scholars, daily items and animals. Very often, they expressed the people's wish for a good life.

Wuxi is well-known for its clay figurines of little children. Emperor Qianlong travelled to Mount Huiquanshan on his Jiangnan tour and encountered a clay figurine master called Wang Chunlin. The latter could make exquisite clay figurines. Qianlong then ordered him to make five plates of clay children. The emperor bestowed on him beautiful gold plates and gold silk and satin. From then on, clay figurines of little children from Wuxi became widely known.

Clay Figurines and Folk Customs
Praying for a son with clay figurines

In some parts of China, temples would prepare clay dolls to be offered before an image of a god.

Childless women would hang round a clay doll a red thread with a coin token inscribed with Longevity. The act symbolised that they had grabbed hold of a son.

Worshipping the Moon
In Beiping, every family had to set up an altar to pray to the moon on the 15th day of the eighth lunar month. The children loved to play with clay rabbits at that time. It was believed to usher in good fortune and remove all ailments.

Next, they would bring the clay doll home in a red cloth and place it next to their ancestors' tablets.

Praying for Rain
In olden days, clay dragons kneaded by children were also used in praying to Heaven for rain. At the same time, the people would sing this song: "Green Dragon Head, White Tiger Tail, Heaven loves it when children pray for rain…"

Clay Dogs

Clay dogs were exaggerated and interesting. They looked like a dog and a monkey at the same time. Most outstanding was its feminine quality. That expressed the Chinese emphasis on perpetuating the family lineage. From the second day of the second month until the third day of the third month, the Huaiyang people of He'nan would pray to their ancestors. Farmers would bring baskets of clay dogs to sell at the temples.

Clay dogs (*ninigou* 泥泥狗) are not just confined to dogs. They also include other animals. A better-known version is the tiger.

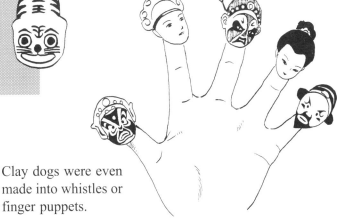

Clay dogs were even made into whistles or finger puppets.

A-fu

A-fu, a symbol of diligence, kindness, honesty and helpfulness, is a clay figurine from Wuxi that is known far and wide.

A-fu came from a poor family. Her mother died after giving birth to her.

My child's mother! My child's mother!

No disaster is a blessing to the poor.

My ill-fated child, you're born motherless.

I'll call you A-fu*. I hope Heaven will protect you from harm.

A-fu's father had to be away on business. So he married another woman to take care of A-fu.

After giving birth to a son, A-fu's stepmother pushed many household chores to A-fu.

A-fu, there is no water in the vat. Go and fetch some water!

*Fu 福 is good fortune.

106

No matter how her stepmother treated her, A-fu would always wear a smile on her face.

She's really a good child. She's filled my water vat again.

When I fall ill, she'll even pick medicinal herbs for me.

Boy, where are you going?

I'm going over there to play. I'll be back soon.

Mother won't let Sister eat. Sister won't have the strength to cut the firewood on an empty stomach.

I'm going to bring her this biscuit.

Roar!

Argh! Tiger!

Run Brother!

Please save my sister!

A-fu!

A-fu!

Look! It's A-fu's tattered clothes.

This mud is stained with A-fu's blood. I'm going to use it to make a clay figurine of A-fu.

This is Ah-fu.

Other villagers who missed A-fu also started making clay figurines of her. From that day onwards, Wuxi began to produce clay figurines of A-fu which became very popular.

Dough Modelling

There is another kind of modelling handicraft which uses dough. It began in the Tang Dynasty and has been around for 1,000 years. Dough modelling uses flour as its main ingredient. In the beginning, farmers' wives would use dough to create fruit, flowers and animals while preparing flour products. After steaming them, they added some food colouring. These figurines were both edible and decorative. As the art form developed, dough modelling was soon detached from noodles and rice to become an art in itself.

The Origin of Dough Figurines

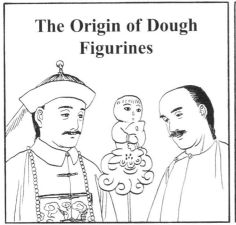

Liu Yong was an official in Beijing during Emperor Qianlong's reign in the Qing Dynasty.

What a unique steamed bun! I really can't bear to eat it.

Old Wang, where did you learn this art from?

Your Excellency, I come from a poor family. I can't afford to give out snacks during festive periods.

So I kneaded the dough into various shapes before steaming them. I then gave them away as gifts. Everybody likes them.

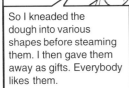

Are you able to knead the Eight Immortals for me?

Let me give it a try.

Old Wang kneaded the figurines with dough and added some colours to them.

If you add some honey in the dough, it will keep longer.

In addition, adding colours to the dough and steaming them separately before you knead them will create a more exquisite image.

I'm sure you'll be able to sell them.

I'll do as Your Excellency says.

Your Excellency, it's done.

Wow! It's just like ivory carving.

Old Wang, His Majesty's birthday is coming. Knead the Eight Immortals and God of Longevity as gifts from me to His Majesty.

Ha! Ha! Excellent!

Who made them? Such intricate skills!

This gift beats the rest hands down.

I'm willing to pay him a lot of gold to make another set of the Eight Immortals.

Here. I'll make you the Monkey God.

I want to be a dough figurine maker when I grow up.

Old Wang's name spread far and wide henceforth. He then switched to making dough figurines for a living. Old Wang passed his skills down to his son and students. And so the art was passed down the generations.

The Legend of Nüwa

Clay and dough modellers hold three emperors in awe, namely Tianhuang (Heavenly Emperor), Dihuang (Earth Emperor) and Renhuang (Human Emperor). But it is also believed that the three emperors refer to Fuxi, Nüwa and Shennong. The story about Nüwa making clay figurines remains the most famous.

When the Earth was first formed, there was no Mankind on Earth. The place was desolate.

What a vast land. But there is no life form on it. It's so quiet.

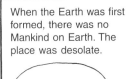

Let's make a clay figurine based on my image.

Let's add the mouth and the nose.

Wait! Don't run about!

You're not completed!

One clay figurine will be too lonely. Let me make a few more so that this world will be more lively.

The clay figurines then went on their separate ways and headed off in different directions. Soon, they were spread all over the world.

Using my hands to make them is too slow.

She then dipped a rope in wet clay and, with a flick of the rope, the clay globs also turned into clay figurines.

But these clay figurines were not as fine as those made with hands. Some had no arms and some, no legs. They became the crippled people.

Ha! I found a tassel on the rope.

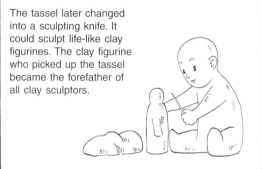

The tassel later changed into a sculpting knife. It could sculpt life-like clay figurines. The clay figurine who picked up the tassel became the forefather of all clay sculptors.

One day, the sky collapsed.

I created them! How could I let them suffer?

Nüwa then found some coloured stones. After burning them, she used them to fill the hole in the sky.

Making colourful clay figurines is the figurine makers' way of imitating Nüwa's act of plugging holes in the sky with coloured stones.

PAPER CUTTING

Paper cutting involves cutting holes out of paper to create beautiful works of art. This art form goes a long way back. Excavated ivory, bones and earthenware belonging to the New Stone Age were found to have carvings which seemed to be done with the method of paper cutting.

Before paper was invented, pictures were cut from leather, cotton cloth and silver foil. They could be considered the precedent to paper cutting. After the Eastern Han Period, when paper-making grew substantially, paper cutting as a folk art was born.

These carvings were found on wares from the New Stone Age.

Two Types of Paper Cutting

Patterned cut
There are fewer holes in this paper design.

Monochrome cut
More holes are cut out in this design.

Various Uses of Paper Cuttings

Door paper Cuttings

They are pasted during New Year celebrations. Paper cuttings of the Guardian God and phrases like *lao shao ping an* 老少平安 (all is well) and *gong xi fa cai* 恭喜发财 (wealth and prosperity) are pasted on the door.

Window paper Cuttings

Paper cuttings symbolising good fortune will be pasted on windows during New Year and wedding celebrations. New homes are also pasted with window paper cuttings. They lend a touch of celebratory air.

Furniture Paper Cuttings

They are pasted on crockery, cabinets, tea tables and mirrors.

Embellishment

They are used to decorate birthday, wedding or New Year gifts for friends and relatives.

Themes for Paper Cuttings

There is no limit to the themes and subjects. Anything goes for paper cutting. Below are some examples of the more commonly seen ones:

They express auspicious meanings like many offspring and celebration.

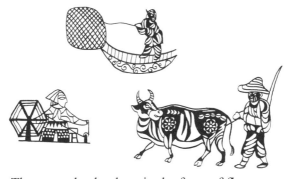

They can also be done in the form of flowers, grass, worms, birds, scenery and lanterns.

Others depict scenes from folklore and history such as Madam White Snake and Wu Song Killing the Tiger.

How a Paper Cutting is Done

You need a pair of scissors and a few pieces of paper to do a paper cutting. If you want to create more complicated patterns, you'll need a carving knife.

The paper used should be ideally thin but firm. If it's too tough, cutting it won't be easy. If it's too flimsy, it will crumple easily.

Cutting out the Pattern

Step 1: Fold the paper into equal parts to form rectangles.

Step 2: Draw the pattern on the paper.

Edge

Centre fold

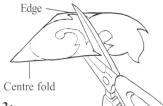

Step 3:
Cut out the parts that have been marked.
Cut from the centrefold away from the edge of the paper. Otherwise, the paper would split into several pieces.

Step 4: Unfold the paper when it is done and there you have it, a beautiful border.

The Story of Yangzhou Paper Cutting

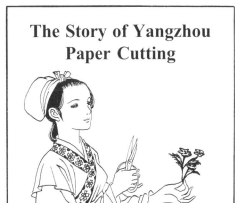

There was a girl who lived in Yangzhou. She made a living from selling paper cuttings.

Mister, buy a paper cutting.

Looks ordinary.

Look, that old lady over there makes very vivid paper cuttings. Her skills are superb!

I want one too!

Me too!

The pair of scissors is so rusty.

Another year passed by…

Ah! This pair of scissors is as good as new!

Good skills take one places. Crowds will come for her paper cuttings.

The garden and the house are gone. Where's Granny?

That is Granny's voice!

Ah! Granny must be a deity!

This pair of scissors is fantastic. The flower that I want to cut out will just come to my mind in a flash.

From then onwards, the girl's paper cuttings became very popular. She also took in many disciples and passed her skills down the generations.

CHINESE KNOT ORNAMENTS

Heart to heart we are bound closely
The knot of love is to be tied tightly.
It's time now to part with each other,
Yet we linger long, hard to separate.
Tied, I will remain your faithful wife,
Tied, Sir, when will you come back?
Merely a dressing ornament, I once thought,
It has linked two hearts, now I see.
Wearing it while walking or resting,
I hope it'll bring us a hundred years of love.
— Meng Jiao (751-814 AD), "A Knot of Love."

This is a classical Chinese poem dedicated to the Chinese knot. The Chinese knot is a symbol of strength, harmony, unity, and love between men and women. These symbolic meanings are embedded in many Chinese phrases containing the Chinese character for knot (*jie*) such as "*jie he* (come together), *jie hun* (get married), *tuan jie* (be united), *jie guo* (bear fruit, give birth to children), *jie fa fu qi* (husband and wife by first marriage), *yong jie tong xin* (two hearts tied up forever). *Jie* is also a partial homophone of *ji* (lucky or auspicious) that is closely associated with such Chinese characters as *fu* (happiness), *lu* (joy or salary), *shou* (longevity), *cai* (wealth), *xi* (delight), *an* (peace), and *kang* (health). That is why the Chinese knot has survived till today as a perfect mascot.

Origin of the Chinese Knot

The Chinese knot became popular in the Tang and Song dynasties, and flourished during the Ming and Qing dynasties. It is still well loved by modern people enjoying the benefits of coffee culture in the Information Age. In the remote past, people made knots with rope to record events. As rope is pronounced almost the same as god in Chinese, there was a period of time in Chinese history when rope was widely worshipped. By the time of the Tang and Song dynasties, rope-made knots had become a type of ornament. The Chinese have developed a habit of wearing ornaments since olden times. Most of these ornaments were tied to their clothes with knotted strings. Ancient Chinese liked to make different ornaments with silk strings for wearing or expressing their best wishes. In the Ming and Qing dynasties, people started to give names to these knot ornaments, which thus acquired even richer meanings.

Features of the Chinese Knot

All Chinese knot ornaments are symmetrical, left and right, and up and down. They are made with one single string. Depending on their symbolic meanings, Chinese knot ornaments fall into two categories: auspicious knot and dressing knot.

Auspicious Knot

Ancient Chinese used to place such ornaments on the curtains in the temple or the monks' cassocks in the hope of warding off the evil and turning misfortune into good fortune. Today people use them to adorn their homes and cars as hanging ornaments. Typical auspicious knot

ornaments include the double-fish knot with four Chinese characters — "*ji qing you yu* (luck, festivity, have, excess)," the *ruyi* knot with "*ji xiang ru yi* (good luck and success)," and other designs with such phrases as "*fu shou shuang quan* (enjoy happiness and longevity)," "*chu ru ping an* (come and go peacefully)" and "*yi lu shun feng* (have a good journey)."

Dressing Knot

These are wearable knot ornaments, including ring, eardrop, bracelet, necklace, belt, and antique belt hook.

How to Make a Chinese Knot?

Required tools:

1. A pair of scissors; 2. A ruler; 3. A piece of foam mat; 4. A set of special crochet hooks; 5. A lighter; 6. A pair of forceps; 7. Transparent spray paint.

Five Steps:

1. Preparing: conceptualise the knot's shape, colour, function and accessories; sketch a model; and prepare materials and tools.
2. Weaving: this process involves a combination of such weaving techniques as threading, reeling, picking and pressing.
3. Pulling: pull the surplus thread to the end to help the knot form.
4. Decorating: decorate, repair, cover up and make up. Usually, to make a knot requires an integration of the above three steps: weaving, pulling, and decorating.
5. Shaping: Turn the knot over with its back facing upwards, and place it on a sheet of white paper. Fetch a bottle of transparent spray paint, shake it even, and spray it onto the knot at a distance of 5 to 10 cm. It takes about four to five hours for the paint to penetrate the knot. The knot then acquires a fixed shape.

RATTAN PRODUCTS

Rattan products are handicrafts made from materials such as rattan stems and core. Being hard, light, and natural in colour, these products combine antiqueness and elegance, qualities that make them a favourite for people down the ages.

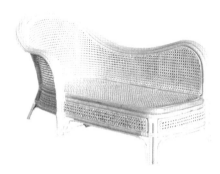

Historical Anecdotes about Rattan Products

Rattans were used to make helmets and armours as early as the period of clan society. By the Western Zhou Dynasty and the Warring States Period, rattan baskets had already become an important civilian means of transport in south China. A legend has it that when Zhuge Liang stationed his troops at Jianmen in northern Sichuan, his men used rattan stems as staffs. This gave rise to the name brand of Jiange rattan staff as well as the saying: "Gold has a price while rattan staffs are priceless."

There is an abundant supply of rattan materials in South China. Rattan products there are cheap and can be seen in each and every household. Common rattan products include rattan cupboards, small rattan tables, long rattan desks, rattan screens, rattan racks, rattan chairs, rattan tables, and rattan beds.

Three provinces famous for rattan products are Fujian Province, Hainan Province and Yunnan Province. In Fujian's Yongfu County, rattan making is a centuries-old craft. Red and white rattans are abundant in Hainan. Tengchong rattan products in Yunnan have a history of more than a thousand years.

Rattan Products across the World

Major rattan producers are located in Indonesia, Africa, India, Vietnam, Malaysia, and the Philippines. Of all Southeast Asian countries, Indonesia is the largest supplier of rattan materials. It is said that Zheng He brought China's rattan-making techniques to this area during his voyages to the western seas.

How to Make Rattan Products?

First step: striking the rattans (removing their nodes);

Second step: selecting, rinsing, and open-air drying the rattans;

Third step: stretching, scratching, bleaching, and dying the rattans;

Fourth step: weaving;

Fifth step: finishing.

Rattan sheets are handmade. Rattan furniture is made from rattan peels, rattan core, and rough rattans.

CARVING

Chinese carving covers a broad spectrum. Below are some examples:

Jade Carving

The Chinese have always loved jade. It is regarded as an auspicious item that wards off disaster. Hence, jade carving started very early. The items included accessories and daily utensils decorated with carvings of flowers, birds, animals and humans. The material used included jade, emerald jade, agate, crystal and others. As jade is very sturdy, a piece of jade sculpture has to be polished for at least one year for the shine to come through.

Stone Carving

They refer to carvings on marble, bluestone, granite and sandstone. Such carvings can be auspicious patterns such as dragon, phoenix, crane, lion, tiger and Kirin. Major suppliers of stone carvings are located in provinces such as Fujian, Guangxi and Shaanxi. The well-known "Shou Shan Stone" from Fujian is often used to carve figures, landscapes and animals. The stone was allegedly used by Nüwa to mend the broken sky!

Ivory Sculpture

Intricate carving of humans, flowers, birds and animals on ivory tusk is its hallmark. The best ivory carving comes from Beijing and Guangzhou.

Wood Carving

It is simple and understated. Wood carving is usually done on practical items or ornaments. The earliest wood carving dates back 7,000 years ago.

Bamboo Carving

Bamboo carving combines the natural beauty of bamboo and art. Humans, landscape, drawings and patterns are carved onto bamboo.

Carving covers a wide area. Besides the abovementioned ones which are better-known, there are also shell mosaic, charcoal carving and coconut-shell carving in China too. And the list does not end here!

Jade sculpture.

Ivory carving.

Wood carving.

Leaf carving.

Shell carving.

Coconut carving.

Sand carving.

Horn carving.

CLOISONNÉ ENAMEL

Cloisonné enamel is a unique form of art. Originating in Beijing, the earliest cloisonné enamel came from the Yuan Dynasty. It has been around for at least 1,000 years. Cloisonné enamel's popularity peaked in the Ming Dynasty. During the Jingtai reign of the Ming Dynasty, artisans discovered a deep blue glaze which made the most beautiful wares. As such, people called the art form *jing tai lan* 景泰蓝.

Cloisonné enamel was exclusive to the royalty. It was a symbol of one's power and status. Cloisonné enamel was found in many items such as containers of worship, crockery, wash basins, etc. It was also seen in furniture and screens. Cloisonné enamelled bangles and earrings also became fashionable accessories. Cloisonné enamel was also commonly given away as gifts.

Making Cloisonné Enamel
1) Bronze forms the base of the utensil or ware
2) The finer bronze strips are pinched to form different patterns.
3) The patterns are welded to the bronze base.
4) Different types of coloured enamel are used to fill in the colour.
5) The piece is then fired a few times to secure the enamel. It is then polished and plated with gold.

WAX DYE

Wax dye is one of the traditional handmade floral printing art forms in China. The minority tribes in the south-western region had already grasped the technique of wax dye way back during the Qin to Han Period. Until today, this skill is still very popular among these people. Wax dye is highly decorative and is favoured on dresses, wall pictures, accessories and table cloths. Wax-dyed cloth has also become fashionable wear.

Wax dye is also popular in Indonesia, Sri Lanka, India and Japan. Each country has its own distinctive style.

A dress made from wax-dyed cloth.

Wax-dyed tapestry.

Wax-dyeing

1) Use wax to outline the drawing of a bird or flower on a piece of white cloth.
2) Once the wax has dried, dip the cloth into a vat of dye (usually blue dye).
3) Use boiling water to remove the wax.
4) The drawing or pattern is revealed on the cloth.

SNUFF BOTTLE

Snuff bottles are used to store powdered tobacco. It is said snuff bottles were an article of tribute from the Italians during the Ming Dynasty.

Though very few people sniffed tobacco in China, artisans were able to use various materials and artistic techniques to turn the traditional medicine bottle into a piece of exquisite art. Snuff bottles became a highly-valued collectible.

There are many designs when it comes to snuff bottles. The process involved is also very complicated. There is the carved design, the embossed design and the one which is hand-drawn on the inside of the bottle. Making intricate carvings and drawings on a small bottle calls for consummate skills. It is definitely a Chinese masterpiece.

Snuff is powdered tobacco mixed with expensive fragrant herbs. It is then left to age inside a wax ball for years or even decades. Snuff comes in various colours. The smell is spicy. It is believed to brighten one's eyes, perk one up and promote blood circulation.

TIGER-HEAD SHOES

It is a kind of children's shoes. As the head of a tiger is sewn onto them, they are called tiger-head shoes. The tiger is widely regarded as a divine beast which wards off evil and keeps one safe. Parents let their children wear tiger-head shoes in the hope that the children will grow up to be healthy.

The designs can be very exaggerated but the workmanship is excellent, and so adults began to look at it as a piece of art.

Besides these shoes, there is also the tiger-head hat. It serves to protect the wearer too.

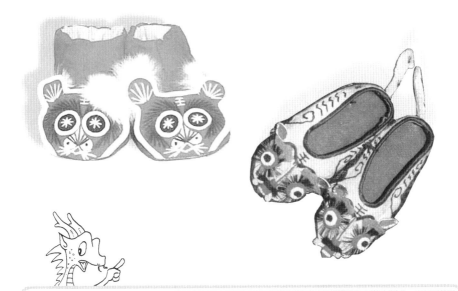

The tiger-head shoes is just one type of animal shoes in China. Children in China have been wearing animal shoes for a long time. They include cat-head shoes, rabbit shoes, lion shoes and even the pig-snout shoes. They are very interesting.

FACIAL MAKE-UP
AND FACE MASK

In Chinese operas, you'll see colourful and exaggerated facial make-up on the performers. The decorative value of facial make-up is outstanding, hence facial make-up is often featured in handmade art pieces. Foreigners especially like to decorate their homes with these handmade pieces.

According to Chinese dramatist Zhang Geng, Chinese facial make-up is a special plastic art used exclusively by traditional Chinese operas in stage performance. As part and parcel of Chinese operas, it serves to reveal the characters' moral qualities.

Chinese facial make-up is a unique part of Chinese opera. Chinese opera has these four characters:

Sheng 生 — a male role, like a young man, an elderly man, a warrior.

Dan 旦 — a female role like a young lady, a beautiful lady, a lady warrior, an elderly woman.

The make-up for *sheng* and *dan* roles should highlight the eyes and eyebrows and the application of rouge. This type of make-up is known as the *sumian* 素面 (plain face).

Jing 净 — also known as the painted face used on a chivalrous and rugged male role.

Chou 丑 — also known as the little painted face used on bad or comical characters.

Jing and *chou* follow a standard way of make-up. It uses different colours and strokes to exaggerate the actors' features, either to beautify them or to make them ugly. They are used to show the personality of the character and to add a touch of drama to the role. This is the Chinese facial make-up that we are familiar with.

Various Kinds of Facial Make-up

Three-part Make-up (*sankuaiwa* 三块瓦)
It emphasises the forehead and cheeks. Used on heroes and warriors.

Worn-out Face (*polian* 破脸)
Also called broken face or old face, the strokes, patterns and
colours used on these faces are more complicated. They express
the character's innermost feelings.

The facial make-up follows a standard
format. You are not allowed to change the
style or look of that character. The colours
are classified as primary, secondary,
peripheral and complementary. No matter
how complicated the make-up may be, there
is always one main colour used to highlight
the role's character.

**The Meaning Behind the Colours
Used in Facial Makeup:**
Red — loyalty and courage
Yellow — cruelty and savagery
Golden yellow — gods and demons
White — evil
Blue — carelessness and impetuousness
Black — righteousness
Green — chivalry

Beancurd Face (*doufukuailian* 豆腐块脸)
A white square is drawn around the nose. It is the facial make-up for a *chou* role.

White Face (*fenbailian* 粉白脸)
White powder is applied all over the face. A black pencil is used to highlight the eyes, brows, nose and muscles. It is used on a cunning role.

Some types of facial make-up come with a beard and moustache.

Famous Examples of Chinese Opera Make-up

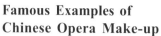

Below are the various types of make-up for familiar literary and opera characters. Do you know them?

Sun Wukong: Monkey God from the Chinese classic *Journey to the West*.

Zhang Fei: A rash and upright general from the Chinese classic *Romance of the Three Kingdoms*.

Justice Bao: A famous magistrate from the Song Dynasty who was impartial and just.

Wu Song: The hero who killed a tiger in the Chinese classic *Water Margin*.

General Guan: A loyal and brave general from the Chinese classic *Romance of the Three Kingdoms*.

The Origin of the Face Mask

Emperor Tang Taizong of the Tang Dynasty liked his officials to perform opera for him.

Wei Zheng, it's now your turn to perform.

Your Majesty, please spare me. It's very embarrassing to perform before so many people.

Let me think of something to help you out.

Wear this face mask to cover your face. You won't feel so awkward then.

Wei Zheng became bolder after putting on the face mask. Over time, this kind of face mask became popular and was called the "official's mask".

But the audience wouldn't be able to see the actors' facial expressions behind the face masks. So the actors began to paint their faces in many different ways. This became known as the Chinese facial make-up.

The Origin of the Beancurd Face

Emperor Tang Minghuang enjoyed watching opera tremendously. He would sometimes take on a role himself.

My dear concubine, what role would you like me to play today?

You're the ruler of the country. You decide.

I do get a little tired from being the emperor at times.

It would be refreshing to play a clown!

Your Majesty, you're so funny! Ha, ha!

And so the Beancurd Face was passed down the generations.

As the emperor had played the *chou* role before, this role gained respect among the opera troupes. Before every performance, the actor playing that role would have to touch all the make-up colours before anyone can use them.

CHINESE FACE MASKS

As an age-old worldwide cultural work, masks are widely used in hunting, combating, sacrifice offering, funerals, dancing, acrobatic and dramatic performance. Facial make-up is done on the face. It is derived from ancient face masks.

Chinese face masks preceded facial make-up. It existed way back in ancient times when the Yellow Emperor battled Chi You. (For more details, please refer to *Origins of Chinese People and Customs*.)

After Chi You died in the battle, he transformed into a beast with huge eyes and a huge mouth. The ancient people wore a mask of the beast in their performance to ward off evil spirits.

Functionally, Chinese masks fall into four categories: sacrificial masks, combating masks, funeral masks and dancing masks.

Various Types of Chinese Face Masks

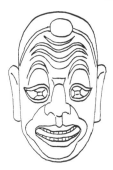

Face Masks for Ghost Plays

Ghost plays were based on a type of sorcery practised in olden days to ward off ghosts and spirits. The masks used were largely those of gods. Strong religious nuances were evident in them.

Face Masks for Local Plays

They have the face, the helmet and and the ears. The carving is exquisite and the colours, dazzling.

Yunnan Face Masks for Suppressing Evil

Tiger Face Masks from Shaanxi

A Bronze Face Mask (Western Zhou period)

Wooden Face Masks from Yunnan

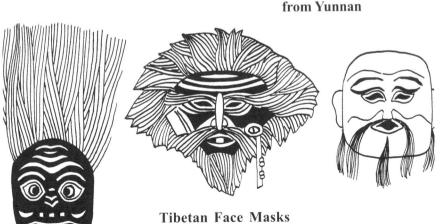

Tibetan Face Masks

The King of Lanling's Face Mask

Ha! Ha! How could you send a girl to fight in a war?

Our king's martial skills are unsurpassable. But he looks too much like a girl.

I doubt we can fight this war now.

Little girl, go home and work on your embroidery! We don't fight with girls.

What can I do to make myself look more imposing?

The king of Lanling found a piece of wood and carved an imposing face on it.

Ah! What a frightening face!

Let's run for our lives!

That was the precedent to the face mask.

UMBRELLA

Umbrellas were seen in China about 2,000 years ago. China is best known for her oilpaper umbrellas and silk umbrellas.

Oilpaper Umbrella

Oilpaper umbrellas from Fujian and Hunan are the best. Flowers, birds and landscapes are handpainted on the umbrella tops. A layer of tung oil is coated on the paper to make it waterproof.

Before the advent of the western umbrella, every family had an oilpaper umbrella. Though it is seldom seen these days, this umbrella, with its rich folk heritage, has been passed down the generations as a piece of folk art.

Silk Umbrella

Hangzhou is famous for its silk umbrellas. The thin silk cover is held by a bamboo frame. Landscapes are often printed on them. Silk umbrellas are light and are very popular with the local ladies as a parasol.

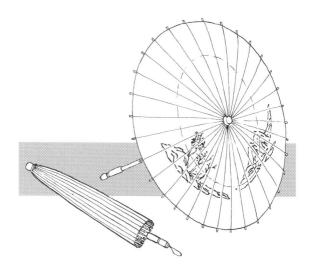

The Symbolism of the Umbrella

Other than providing shade and shelter against the rain and sun and as a form of artistic expression, umbrellas carry other meanings too.

The pronunciation for paper (*zhi*) umbrella sounds like son (*zi*). In Hakka custom, parents give their son an umbrella as he enters adulthood to signify he is a grown-up.

Umbrella (*san*) also sounds like dodge (*shan*). So it means ghosts will dodge it. Hence it is also used to ward off evil spirits.

Umbrella (*san*) also sounds like scatter (*san*). So umbrellas are not opened in the house lest the family falls apart (*san*).

The Origin of the Umbrella

Lu Ban hailed from the Warring States Period. He was a well-known artisan and mason.

One day, Lu Ban and his younger sister visited the West Lake in Hangzhou.

Brother, it's raining!

What a damper!

Brother, you have such deft fingers. You're able to build buildings and mend bridges.

How come there's nothing you can do about this rain?

I have to think of something so that people can still visit the West Lake even when it's raining.

Let's have a contest to see who can create the best tool to avoid rain.

You're on. We'll have one night to decide who the winner is.

This pavilion provides shade and shelter. Sister is going to lose.

Within one night, Lu Ban built nine pavilions next to the West Lake.

The rooster has crowed. Let's stop here.

149

The Legend of Carrying An Umbrella to Ward Off Ghosts

Legend has it that there is a torch of Samadhi Fire on the forehead of a good man. Once this fire shines at a ghost, it will be burnt to eternal hell. The higher the forehead, the stronger the fire.

Hell

Granny, it's cold. Take these two taels of silver to buy a thick cotton-padded jacket.

Mister, you're such a good man.

His life is coming to an end. Bring him back.

That's him!

Lock his neck with the chain and bring him back to Hades.

The two ghosts slid under the umbrella and were scorched and burnt into ashes by his Samadhi Fire.

Ah! It turned out that this man's Samadhi Fire was too strong.

The ghosts did not notice it as the umbrella had hidden it from their view.

Afterwards, whenever children or the sickly had to travel a distance, someone from home would carry an umbrella for them to ward off ghosts. This practice gradually became a custom.

CHINESE CULTURE SERIES
150x210mm, fully illustrated

ORIGINS OF CHINESE PEOPLE AND CUSTOMS
Explores the beginnings of the Chinese people, origins of Chinese names, Chinese zodiac signs, the afterlife, social etiquette and more!

ORIGINS OF CHINESE FESTIVALS
Stories about Lunar New Year, Chinese Valentine's Day, Qing Ming, Dragon Boat, Zhong Yuan, Mid-Autumn Festivals and more.

ORIGINS OF CHINESE CULTURE
Interesting facts about the "Four Treasures of the Study": the brush, ink, paper and inkstone, which form the cornerstone of Chinese culture.

ORIGINS OF CHINESE MARTIAL ARTS
Traces the origins of the *gongfu* of Shaolin and Wudang warriors and their philosophy and chivalry code.

ORIGINS OF SHAOLIN KUNG FU
An entertaining read for all budding martial arts enthusiasts and all who want to explore the wonders of Shaolin Kung Fu!

ORIGINS OF CHINESE CUISINE
Showcases famous and best-relished dishes, including Peking Roast Duck and Buddha Jumps Over the Wall, and the stories behind them.

ORIGINS OF CHINESE FOOD CULTURE
Covers the origins, history, customs, and the art and science of Chinese food culture, including the 18 methods of cooking.

ORIGINS OF CHINESE TEA AND WINE
Tea and wine have a long history in China. In fact, both have become firmly entrenched in the culture and customs of the Chinese people.

ORIGINS OF CHINESE SCIENCE & TECHNOLOGY
Covers great inventions by the Chinese: the compass, paper-making, gunpowder and printing. Also explores Chinese expertise in the fields of geography, mathematics, agriculture and astronomy.

中华手工艺的故事

编著 ： 李小香

绘画 ： 傅春江

翻译 ： 韩 玉与杨立平

亚太图书有限公司出版